To the Best Mom and Dad in the World

YOU ARE A STRONG MAN

YOU ARE A STRONG MAN

Addressing the Pitfalls That Men Face &
Providing Tools To Overcome Them

ROBERT B. VANN

Robert B. Vann
W.C.E. Publishing
5515 Brickell Rd
Norfolk, VA 23502
www.Robertbvann.com
info@robertbvann.com

Printed in the United States of America
First Printing 2019
First Edition 2019
ISBN 978-1-5136-55444

10 9 8 7 6 5 4 3 2 1

TABLE OF CONTENTS

PREFACE

Now, I must tell you. This is not your typical Male self-help book. This is a book packed with much truth, love, funniness, and transparency. Even to the point of mere embarrassment at times, God allowed me to open up and be honest about some vulnerable parts of my life while exposing my silliness and crazy ways.

I speak about some of my greatest moments and some of my worse while tying them all together with God's word and truth. I've learned over the years that friends, family, money, jobs, education, and opportunities can disappear in an instant but the word of God will always remain and be consistent in its effectiveness. Therefore, Throughout this book you will find many scripture references matched with practical life examples that make the content of this book more understandable and relatable to any reader.

So, Why did I write this book?

Honestly, I didn't have a choice. I had to write this book; it saved my life. One Sunday morning, standing in the pulpit with my ministers robe on and a sermon ready to preach, I was ready. Just as I had done countless times before for the last few years. This Sunday was not really that special but there was something different about it. Actually, this particular Sunday my wife wasn't in church with me and actually, she was no longer staying in our home. We had been separated for a while and our marriage was on the verge of divorce. This was a very low place for me, but I decided that I would not stop serving God and his people.

So as the service went on and I participated In praise and worship, I heard God speak to me clear as day and say, " You are a Strong Man." These words hit me so hard because with everything that I was going through, I did not feel like a Strong Man. Actually, I hadn't felt like one for a long time. For years I battled with being separated from my father as a child, being molested, rejected, abandoned, insecurities, low self-esteem, and many other things then to end up with my marriage on the brink of divorce I was stuck. I had nothing to say and nothing to give. So hearing those words I broke down. I laid down and cried because internally I was sad and broken but his words gave me hope.

It was at that moment that I realized that though I was weak, I was also strong. It was at that moment that God challenged me to see beyond my pain and into my promise. Due to that, I started thinking about you and our other brothers around the world who are broken, confused, lost, discouraged, lonely, and just need a little love and support. I started thinking about those men who are stagnant and have settled for what life has given them or still living off of the achievements of old. I started thinking about those fathers who regret the decisions they've made, husbands who feel ashamed, and Pastors who have no strength to lead their churches.

So why did I write this book? I wrote this book to revive a world full of men who are strong but have forgotten their power. I wrote this book to save a man from giving up on himself. I wrote this book to keep a husband from giving up on his wife, a father from leaving his children, a pastor from abandoning his sheep. I wrote this book to push you to stand up again and see yourself as God does. I wrote this book with every intention of sparking a revival in your soul and drawing you closer to Jesus Christ as you soar like an eagle into the destiny that God has called you too. I believe that no man shall be left behind and whether you are a husband, father, leader, student, pastor, businessman, or just a man. This book is for you.

My Sisters Want to Know Too!

One of the most mind blowing things I've learned during the writing process of this book is that many women desire to learn more about men. It was wild to see their responses to the content that I've released, information that I've posted, and talks that I've published. I didn't realize how hungry they are to have a better understanding of their husbands, fathers, sons, uncles, bosses, etc.

It's not because they want to be nosy and manipulate us as men, but because most of us don't talk and share our emotions, they feel left out, confused, and ineffective. They desire to be better wives but don't know how to be better because many of us men don't know how to tell them what we need. They desire to be better mothers, but as sons, we are unable to properly communicate or desires as well. Therefore, if you are one of my amazing sisters reading this book, I say thank you. I say thank you because what you will read in this book is all real, personal, and in your face. There are some very vulnerable and intime moments expressed and if you are able to take them in, your understanding of how a man thinks will enhance and help you be more effective in the lives of men around you.

So please, don't be confused or thrown off by my verbiage or tone of voice in this book because I wrote it directly to men. There may be some things that you won't understand, but while you are reading it, try to view the content and experiences through the lens of the closest man around you. For example, I write about my experience as a husband who was afraid to be without my wife due to my internal struggles with insecurities, abandonment, and rejection. While you're reading about this, think about your husband if you're married, or your boo, babe, if you are single.

I also share in the book about my experience of growing up without my father in the home which made me resent him at times and feel unwanted. If you have a man in your life who has experienced something similar, take some time to build him up by validating his efforts and supporting his pursuits. This may sound like a lot but it will do wonders for him and will take him from simply being a good man to a Strong Man.

Now Sis, I must tell you this: While you are learning more about the experience of strong men, I need you to be a little selfish. The topics in this book range from fatherlessness to Low self-esteem, lack of vision, fear in relationships, confused sexuality, and many other things, so don't just read this book to learn more about men and forsake your ability to be changed as well.

There may be some chapters and experiences in here that you may have had yourself and are still troubling you on the inside, if so, don't be afraid to open up and be vulnerable with us and allow God to strengthen you as well. Allow God to minister to you and bring you healing, deliverance, and freedom because whether you are married, single, a mother, or not, God wants you living life free and in abundance. So sit back and relax and enjoy the ride. You never know, this book may help you be a better wife, mother, or friend, Heck, it might also help you to decipher through all of the men who come at you and discern which one is the Strong Man that God has called you to have.

You are a Strong Man is not a book that is teaching men how to be strong, this is a book that is challenging men to live a Strong Lifestyle. This is not a book to help a man to become better than another one, this is a book that draws men together. This is not a book that exposes a man's weaknesses to his female counterparts, this is a book that bridges the gap and improves their relationships through transparency and truthfulness

So Without a doubt, the fact that you purchased this book is an investment in your life today and your future and you will receive a return on your investment. Feel free to take notes and don't rush through it.

Some chapters will be harder than others but don't give up. Fight through it. Know that God is with you and so are thousands of people around the world who are reading this book with you. You are not alone and your life is not over. It is your time to be Strong! Let's gooooooooooooooooooooo!!!

ROBERT B. VANN

CHAPTER 1
HIDDEN WEAKNESS

<u>2 Corinthians 12: 9</u>

But he said to me, *"My grace is sufficient for you, for my power is made perfect in weakness."* Therefore I will boast all the more gladly about my weaknesses, so that Christ's power may rest on me.

I'm going to be real honest with you sir, it took me a long time to really feel like a strong man. I know that may not have been the best introduction to this chapter but I believe it speaks volumes to the hidden weaknesses that many men face and are plagued with on a daily basis. We spend years trying to be accepted, get jobs, mold our bodies, amass great amounts of success, and fit the parameters of what society says a man should be, but few of us are being successful in our efforts. Because of this, many men struggle with deep insecurities such as the feelings of inadequacy, shame, regret, low self-esteem, doubt, rejection, and abandonment and are hiding these feelings within for fear of being rejected or deemed as being a weak man. Therefore, this chapter will discuss the consequences of fostering hidden weaknesses while comparatively providing practical steps to overcome them and how to use them for your natural and spiritual gain.

Growing up no one ever knew about my fear of approaching girls, fear of rejection, fear of success, and the fear of being misunderstood. I hid these things as a teen in order to maintain a certain reputation unaware of the fact that I would begin to create a system of thinking that would hinder me in my later years as an adult. Growing up as men, most of us are either directly or indirectly taught that men aren't supposed to be weak. Some of us were even taught that real men aren't supposed to show weakness but are supposed to be dominant and strong at all times.

If you are one of these men, I'm sure that this way of life has been tiring and very demanding for you. It's this type of ideology that causes one to work beyond their limit, lift beyond their ability, and prove beyond their capacity, ending up developing problems with their health because they have overworked their bodies trying to uphold a standard that was not realistic. I tell you today sir that you no longer have to have the answers to everything. You no longer have to be strong for everybody and fight for the causes of others while your life is in shambles. Know that God loves you and has more in store for your life than what you have experienced; so let's start from the beginning.

The Beginning

"REAL MEN DON'T CRY", "STOP ALL OF THAT WHINING, BE A BIG BOY", "YOU'RE ALRIGHT, GET UP!" These are examples of what many of us heard growing up that molded our ideology about manhood today. Many of us were even raised to show no emotion at all, and if we showed even a little emotion we were chastised and ridiculed. How has that affected you today? These things affected me greatly, and with no man consistently present in my life to teach me how to properly express my emotions, I taught myself to internalize my pain and refuse to show any weaknesses. I assumed that if I were to show my emotions I would be deemed as weak. Even in my marriage, I would refuse to show my weaknesses because I didn't want my wife to see me struggle or incapable of protecting her.

Through this insecurity, I once asked her if she felt protected around me. It wasn't that I was looking for her to answer in a fashion that would reassure my confidence, but the truth was that I had to ask because I didn't feel that I was capable of protecting her myself. Therefore, if she were to answer in an affirming manner I would've been shocked.

It seems that in today's society you either have to be a macho man with huge muscles or a hard-working man that brings home the bacon to be considered as a man. Especially in order to be accepted by the opposite sex, we have to have a college degree, 6-figure income, 720 credit score, car, house, 5-year plan, puppy, and a decent looking profile picture. Now I must say, all of things are necessary and important, but what if you don't have all of these things? What if you're a man that hasn't attained that 6-figure job, but has a job making minimum wage and is working hard for a promotion? What if you don't have a 6 pack but you're confident with your dad bod?

What I'm proposing is that you don't have to have all of these things to be considered a man, actually you don't need them at all because external things don't validate who you are, God does and has. In the beginning God made you in his image and in his likeness and he fashioned you after himself, so be encouraged and thank God for what you have and who you are today.

Acknowledge Your Weaknesses

I'm going to say something that you probably haven't heard from a lot of people, but here it is: Real Men Are Weak. Yes, I said it, Real men are Weak. Please, let me explain before you give up on this book.

First, weakness is defined as the state or condition of lacking strength. This lack of strength is not just practically speaking of your physical strength but it also pertains to your emotional and spiritual strength as well. The Apostle Paul in 2 Corinthians 12: 9(NIV) writes about his weaknesses this way by saying, "But he said to me, "My grace is sufficient for you, for my power is made perfect in weakness. Therefore, I will boast all the more gladly about my weaknesses, so that Christ's power may rest on me." At first glance, this is a hard truth to practice because not only does this scripture show that he not only acknowledged his weaknesses but he boasted about them and allowed God to overshadow them with his power.

See a few scriptures before this one Paul explains how he asked God three times to take his thorn away from him. The thorn in this case, was a messenger from satan that was sent to torment him to prevent him from becoming prideful. See a thorn can be anything that you face repeatedly that makes you weak, drained, or insufficient as a man and sometimes you may feel that you have multiple. I've felt that I had multiple thorns to include doubt, low self-esteem, lack of confidence, fear, and anxiousness, but I've learned that most of these things aren't my thorn. They are able to torment me due to my unwillingness to let them go which is a sign of pride. Therefore, just as Paul stated, a thorn is not sent to destroy you, a thorn is sent to keep you humble and before the face of God.

So let me ask you, what is your thorn? What is it that you have been asking God to take away from you and it seems that it will never leave you alone? What vice, addiction, character trait, fear, or desire have you been pleading with God to remove from your life in order for you to walk in your wholeness but it seems that it will always be a part of who you are?

It is important to acknowledge and identify these weaknesses because they not only affect how we see ourselves but they also affect our relationships with God. Comparatively, due to my constant battle of low self-esteem, God could bless and use me to do great things and I would still feel shameful. Things could be going good and everybody around me could be happy, but as soon as something would go wrong, I would automatically blame myself for the decline of the positive atmosphere of those around me.

Where do our hidden weaknesses come From?

1. Lack of Accomplishment/Completion

Most men have a hidden drive in them to start and complete tasks. We love to work hard and get our hands dirty. Especially when we have something that we really want or a project that looks challenging, our natural reaction is to dominate, control, and overcome. However, this type of domineering attitude can show up in various ways. We act like this in relationships, leadership roles, job opportunities, civic opportunities, daily interactions, and even with our kids. Have you ever bought your child a toy or a game system and somehow took over the game because of your competitive nature? If so, that's okay it happens, however, it speaks to our innate ability to achieve and overcome.

Comparatively, there can be many downfalls to this attitude when a man works hard and competitively strives to be successful in an endeavor and doesn't succeed. There is nothing worse than a man who puts his heart and everything he has into something and it doesn't work out. His frustration isn't only in the fact that he didn't succeed, but he's frustrated because he personally feels that his inadequacy is what caused that project, degree, relationship, parenting, or event not to work out.

Patrick Morley, author of the book Pastoring Men: What works, what doesn't, and why men's discipleship matters now more than ever provides insight on this concept by saying, "So what do men want? When I was younger, I had a long list. Over the years I've whittled my list down to three things. I realize that all taxonomies are imperfect summaries, yet when men find a cause, a companion, and a conviction, everything else generally falls into line" (2016,

p. 52). In this text Morley ends his message by saying that men generally all desire three things: a cause, companion, or conviction. A cause relates to one's purpose or reason for being; while a companion is any loved one, and a conviction being a system that governs one's life. For men, we all need and desire these things, however, the absence of these things in our lives makes us experience deep levels of insecurity and shame that cannot be described and if not addressed can cause us years of hurt, pain, and instability.

2. Comparison and Lack of Personal Vision

One of the greatest hindrances that we face as men is comparing ourselves to other men, whether we perceive them to be more influential than us or more attractive, smart, physically fit, outgoing, or financially stable. On the flip side of that, we often compare ourselves to those we perceive to be weaker, less attractive, accepted, threatening, physically fit, or educated. This practice has become more common in society today because of the great emergence of various social media platforms. Due to the high usage of social media and the time spent on these search engines, it has become nearly impossible for anyone to go a day without scouring a picture, video, or post on social media while consciously or subconsciously measuring themselves to the images and information that they see.

Writers of the article titled Social Comparison, Social Media, Self-esteem titled these two differing comparisons as upward and downward comparisons and explain their effects in our lives in various ways. In their article they write, "Upward social comparison occurs when comparing oneself with superior others who have positive characteristics, whereas downward social comparison occurs when comparing oneself with inferior others who have negative characteristics (Wills,1981;Wood, 1989). Although upward comparison can be beneficial when it inspires people to become more like their comparison targets

(Lockwood & Kunda, 1997), it more often causes people to feel inadequate, have poorer self-evaluations, and experience negative affect (Marsh & Parker, 1984;Morse & Gergen, 1970;Pyszczynski, Greenberg, & LaPrelle, 1985). (p. 206)".

I present this very point because it is very important to see the damage of comparing oneself to another, whether it is via social media or through one-on-one physical interactions. This is a natural occurrence in all of us and can be controlled if you acknowledge how comparison is active in your life and understand how it has affected you until this point. However, to go deeper, I would like to suggest to you that the cause of your comparison can be traced to the lack of possession of a personal vision or plan for yourself. The bible writes about this truth by saying, "Where there is no vision, the people perish: but he that keepeth the law, happy is he" (Proverbs 29: 18, KJV). This scripture exposes the direct effects of a lack of vision in one's life. As it states, if a person doesn't have vision they will perish.

That word perish in this scripture is defined in Hebrew as para' which means to be naked, refuse, uncover set at nought, bare, go back, be loosened of restraint. This basically means that those who don't have vision for their own lives are uncovered and bound to live life according to their past experiences, forsaking the possibilities of their future while living without self-control. With this in mind, it is no wonder why those who don't have a vision are constantly comparing themselves to others and are always talking about the good ole days, simply because, they haven't sought God to figure out what the vision of their future looks like. Therefore, the lack of vision is a hidden weakness that men cover up in many different ways that can be detrimental, but can be solved by seeking God and asking him to give them vision for their future, believing that he will and that they can fulfill it when he shows it to them.

Getting Rid of the Dead Weight

As I stated before, we all have thorns, but there are some things that we have the ability to get rid of with the help of God so let me give you a few examples. First we're going to talk about D.O.U.B.T. (Destroying Our Useless Behavior of Thinking). God gave me this acronym back in 2012 and was beginning to teach me a lesson about my patterns of negative thinking. I didn't realize it at the time, but I was my own thorn. My thoughts created cycles of uncertainty, unbelief, and insecurity which allowed doubt to exist. However, as time would progress I would learn that doubt could no longer live in a person who believes and has faith in God.

See my problem was that I would compare myself to others, try to please them, and rely on their affirmation so much that what they said had more weight than God's word. Looking back now I see how foolish I was and how much God could've done through and for me, but because I wouldn't let go of my perception of myself and accept His, His hands were tied and unable to work in my life. I was so devoted to pleasing others that I failed to please God.

The pressure of pleasing others can be so debilitating that a strong man can lose his strength and give up on life and his relationship with God forever because of the constant feeling of failure and inadequacy. Hebrews 12: 1(NIV) says, "Therefore, since we are surrounded by such a great cloud of witnesses, let us throw off everything that hinders and the sin that so easily entangles. And let us run with perseverance the race marked out for us". So at this moment, if you know that you struggle with doubt, feelings of inadequacy, or the desire to please others take time to pray this prayer:

Lord, thank you for loving me, dying for me, and rising from the dead to intercede for me. I wouldn't be who I am without you but Lord I'm a sinner; please forgive me for my sins. I know that you have brought me out of darkness and into the marvelous light, help me to see the light that you have placed in me and help me to believe in myself. You have not given me a spirit of fear, but of power, love, and a sound mind, so God in the name of Jesus, restore unto me the Joy of my salvation, and Help me to see me as You see me and I will no longer think of myself in a negative way. In Jesus name I pray, Amen.

Dead weight such as doubt, low self-esteem, addictions, lust, perversion, and other things have a way of bringing us down and making us feel inadequate, however, after we have acknowledged these things and given them to God, we are able to live a life of freedom and walk in a life of abundance. As I sit upstairs in my bed and my wife is sleeping downstairs on the couch, after having a conversation listening to her say that "If I had stood up for her, our marriage wouldn't be in the position that it is in," I realize something. I couldn't, because there were times that I couldn't stand up for myself. Now, however, I realize that standing up for oneself doesn't come in building confidence in one's ability to stand, but In understanding that God has already stood up and won every battle we could ever face.

I share this personal truth with you because I want to save you from what I am in the midst of right now. With my marriage on the verge of divorce I'm writing to you to say that you no longer have to hide your weaknesses and God is able to heal you from all things. God is able to deliver you from every hurt, pain, and situation that you have ever and will ever go through.

So please believe me when I say your weaknesses are the key to your greatest strengths and your ability to overcome them through the power of God will empower you to do things that you never would've been able to do. In 1 Corinthians 2: 3-5(NIV) Paul says, "I came to you in weakness with great fear and trembling. My message and my preaching were not with wise and persuasive words, but with a demonstration of the Spirit's power, so that your faith might not rest on human wisdom, but on God's power." Look at his stance, he exposes that he had weaknesses and struggled with fear, however, he didn't allow those things to hinder his ability to serve God. Therefore, he relied on the power of the Holy Spirit for everything

So I say this to you sir. Rely on the Holy Spirit for everything. If there is anything that you are struggling with, ask the Holy Spirit to help you. Romans 8: 26, explains this by saying, "In the same way, the Spirit helps us in our weakness. We do not know what we ought to pray for, but the Spirit himself intercedes for us through wordless groans." So believe me my brother, you don't have to stay the way you are. God truly wants to help you in this journey of life and is willing to walk with you if you let him and tell him exactly what your feeling.

The Freedom of Confession

Before I breakdown this point, I first want to show you through the word of God how much power is in confession:

1 John 1:9 New Living Translation (NLT)

9 But if we confess our sins to him, he is faithful and just to forgive us our sins and to cleanse us from all wickedness.

James 5:16 New Living Translation (NLT)

16 Confess your sins to each other and pray for each other so that you may be healed. The earnest prayer of a righteous person has great power and produces wonderful results.

Proverbs 28:13 New Living Translation (NLT)

13 People who conceal their sins will not prosper,

but if they confess and turn from them, they will receive mercy.

Reviewing these verses, do you see the power in confession? Do you see how God responds to those who confess their faults? God thrives off of confession and actually, the only way to receive Jesus Christ as your personal Lord and Savior is through confession. Therefore, confession is good for your soul and positions you to be blessed. So if you don't have anyone that you can share your deepest and darkest feelings with, talk to God, I promise he would love to listen to you. However, if you have a brother or sister that you can trust; take the time to talk to them and tell them what's on your heart.

Though I promote you to share your weaknesses to your brother or sister, please know that they may not be able to give you an answer to help you. However, as God listens to you confess your weaknesses he already has your answer, he's just waiting on you to trust him with it. God is like the homeboy we all dream of. He will never snitch on you, tell your girlfriend what happened the other night, or slip up and tell your wife what happened during your bachelor party. God is a good guy and desires for his sons to feel comfortable talking to him, but many sons can't speak to God because we are filled with pride.

Pride not only hinders our success but disconnects us from God. Pride was the exact thing that got lucifer kicked out of heaven. It's almost sad to think about how pride has consumed men all over the world, and for most of us, it's not our fault. Growing up we were taught to be prideful, taught to toughen up, not to cry, not to be weak, or have emotions. Most of us were groomed to be silent and to resent our emotions. Well I tell you right now, in order for you to be who God calls you to be, you have to trust Him with your heart, your life, your everything, and you will find that with your transparency with him everything in your life will come into alignment. Trust Him with your weaknesses and watch Him turn you into a Strong Man.

CHAPTER 2
THE FEAR OF CONFLICT

"Don't live in fear to prevent failure, but in faith to attain Success!"

-Robert B. Vann

Handling confrontation can either make or break a man due to the courage that is required and the assault one may receive for doing it. Whether you are a leader, husband, CEO, Pastor, Civil Leader, or father you will experience varying degrees of confrontation. This could range from developing a vision, creating a safe and positive environment in our workplaces, cultivating the gifts of our employees, guiding children, and supporting our wives. Though these things can be tough, one of the most challenging things that I've ever had to face was confronting myself. Now I know this may be rare for a man to admit but I hated confrontation. Even when I saw confrontation coming or a conflict arising I would find a reason to avoid having to be around once the confrontation ensued. It was even to the point that the thought of confronting an issue would paralyze me with fear and fill me with anxiety. Therefore, in this chapter I'm going to share some of my personal experiences with dealing with confrontation and how I overcome it, while also sharing how confrontation can positively affect your life and the benefits it can have in your life and others.

My First Time

It's not a good feeling when a son believes that he is the root of his parents separation or divorce. I felt that way for a long time because of one moment. I remember it like it was yesterday: one night while my parents and I were living in Lawton, Oklahoma I came home and told my mother that my father and I had just left a lady's house that I didn't know. Not knowing who this lady was and being uncertain for why we were even there I told my mother. I didn't know better, I was a child, but after I told her my parents began to immediately argue.

This had been my 1st time ever seeing them argue or even have a disagreement so as I sat in my room scared and confused, I was afraid. After a few months, my father was ordered to transfer and we eventually moved to Columbus, Georgia and things looked like they were going to get better but they didn't. My parents would later separate for a couple years and eventually get divorced after 20 years of marriage and deep down I believed this happened because of me opening my mouth years before. That was the night that I became afraid of confrontation because it seemed to bring about nothing but problems, separation, hurt, and pain. So as a teen and young adult, I avoided confrontation at all cost.

As a child, I became a yes man and was friends with everyone in order to be accepted. I did this so that I would not have to fight or deal with confrontation because I saw how destructive it was in my life and the hurt it caused. This mentality helped me gain a lot of friends, home boys, and comrades, but it did little to nothing for my confidence. Though I was the cool guy and one that all would want to be around, deep down I felt dead and unproductive.

I say this because I didn't have a problem confronting issues for the betterment of other people but I had a problem with confronting issues that pertained to my own well-being.

Out of the 30 years of my life, I've never been in a physical altercation or fight. I've never been punched, slapped, or skull dragged, but there have been many people who have wanted to fight for me. So in 1 instance it seems amazing that I've made it through life without having to fight but on the other hand I wonder why these people desired to fight for me? Was it that they just loved to fight? Was it that they just had my back? Or, was it that they felt sorry for me? I don't really know why they fought for me back then but I do know that as an adult, people have decided to fight for me because I didn't know how to fight for myself. Not only did I not know how to fight for myself but a lot of times I didn't even know I was under attack or being mistreated. Even deeper than that, It wasn't that I didn't know how to physically fight my battles the truth is that I just didn't see anything in me worth fighting for.

See it's hard to fight someone or to ask someone to stop disrespecting you if you don't even know that you're being disrespected. It's even more severe when you're being mistreated and because of your low self-esteem you would rather accept the negative treatment than speak up and get your freedom. This may seem like something that is not common for us to face but if you be honest with yourself you may be able to recollect times when you were mistreated, abused, or disrespected and you chose not to speak up. If not feel free to skip to the next chapter, however, if so, think if there have been times in your life when you may have settled for mistreatment rather than standing up for yourself.

This mistreatment could be physical, emotional, psychological, or spiritual. You know those moments when someone says that you are a failure. Or a time when a close family member touched you in an inappropriate way, or even when you were misled by a church leader who would later drop you to pursue other things. These situations are detrimental to our overall health and if we don't express how we feel and pray, we will fall victim to this type of treatment over and over again.

Thinking about this makes me think of a young man named David who can be found in 1st Samuel chapter 16 and 17. David was a young boy who was assigned to shepherd his father's sheep while his older brothers were warriors and statesmen in King Saul's army. They were known for their stature and impressive fighting skills but David was merely known as a shepherd boy. In this passage we don't get much background about David's upbringing, relationship with his brothers, or even his relationship with his father, but we are given a few hints about their perspective towards him.

In these bible chapters we find a prophet named Samuel who was called by God to go to Jesse's house to anoint the new king of Israel. Now Jesse was David's father, who had 7 other sons that would later be mentioned in the story, but on Samuels way God ensured that Samuel would find Jesse and all of his sons would be present. Upon arrival to Jesse's home, Prophet Samuel asked Jesse to bring out all of his sons in order for him to anoint the new king and Jesse proceeded to bring out his sons 1 by 1. He brought out his first son whose name was Eliab and then his second son and then the third. After assessing the first 3 sons and Samuel denying them all as king, Jesse continued until he had shown his 7 sons. 1 Samuel 16:11 of The Message Bible continues the dialogue between Prophet Samuel and Jesse by saying this, "Then he asked Jesse, "Is this it? Are there no more sons?" "Well, yes, there's the runt. But he's out tending the sheep."

Reading this verse I asked myself, why did Jesse call David a runt? Why couldn't he have called David by name. Then I realized that it is this type of language and environment that breeds low self-esteem and confusion in the life of a young man because if a father doesn't respect the son or isn't present, he won't learn how to respect himself. This is especially true for me because even though I had a great mother growing up who worked and provided everything that I would ever needed, I always missed and desired my father. It wasn't that my father was deadbeat or one who abandoned my mom and I, he was out serving our country as a soldier in the United States Army who retired after more than 20 years of service. Due to his military service, constant deployments, and transfers, my mom and father decided it would be better for my well-being to stay put in Columbus, GA and allowed him to transfer without us as we got settled and rooted in one place.

Though this was apparent at the time, I was never complete until I heard the voice of my father. By my father not being around, it made me believe that if I wasn't good enough for him to be around I wasn't good at all. You may not have had the same situation that I had but there are many things that program our minds to feel less than or unworthy and if you aren't careful, it will cause you to be capable to fight but unable to carry it out due to how you feel within.

Husband Confrontations

It's hard for a man to bounce back from a sequence of consistent weak moments and it's even harder for us to admit that we've had them. After years and internal conflict I can admit that I kind of ran my ex-wife away. I didn't know how to be a king and honestly was scared to try. I was completely terrified of my wife and would tremble in her presence when we were alone. There would be times that I would rather be around others instead of going home and I would even tremble at the notion of praying with her because of the fear of rejection and not being good enough. Now this wasn't always the case and I was but there were times were I would nearly be paralyzed with fear. With this type of emotional storm going on in me, I see now that my instability and double mindedness provided the environment wherein fear and weakness could survive simultaneously. When it came down to my wife, I would give her anything that she wanted or rack my brain trying to figure out how to get it.

I was so dedicated to making her happy that I placed myself on the back burner. This was not healthy for me at all because when she would say certain things or not say, or do certain things or not do them, I would be hurt. I would be so discouraged some days that I would rather stay at the gym for hours on end instead of coming home and facing her. I was an emotional wreck but no one would ever know because I would find a way to cook, clean, wash clothes, wash cars, put gas in her car, help her with her school work, assist during basketball season, teach, preach, serve, and many other things.

Though I was hurting, I ignored my pain, hoping that serving her would eventually make her love me back or make me happy. So how did I get to this point; I became this way when I began to chase my wife instead of lead her. I became a weak husband when my love turned to desperation and every day I came home anticipating divorce papers. So I share this with you to warn you and to expose you to my truth in order for you to redefine yours. By me not confronting how I truly felt in my marriage, it positioned me to live a less than life and one without happiness.

The truth that I've come to understand: The result of me being a fearful husband and my marriage ending in a divorce was not the cause of my wife's actions. The root of fear and instability was due to unresolved issues of my past. Sir, please understand this because a marriage or any close relationship is one of the greatest environments that will expose who you really are. Additionally, relationships are one of the greatest mechanisms that God uses to develop people, therefore, the fears and anxiety that surfaced during my marriage were only a reflection of what was going on within the 13 year old Robert that was trying to do grown up things.

Instead of dealing with my fear, anxiety, shames, and experiences, I got married on top of them. Instead of dealing with my insecurities, I got married in order to heal them. Therefore, If you are in a serious relationship seeking to get married or already married, take some time to search your pain. If you struggle with confronting yourself about your true feelings and emotions it will be even harder to address your feelings and emotions with someone else that you love who also offends you, but you can do it!

Fearful Leader

How many times have you seen something wrong in your workplace, home, church, or community but you didn't address it? Something within you desired to confront it or to stand up for what was right but you didn't. I open with this because as leaders, there are many times we face this type of pause but I've come to learn that this pause can cause major damage to your family, church, business, or community. As a leader in my local church, I assumed that because we all loved God there would be no problems. We all would get along and no one would disagree but boy was I wrong. It seemed that people in the church were more confrontational than people in politics, lol.

Now that may seem like a stretch to some but try to ask some Christians which baptism is right and watch the fight begin. I began to learn that at the center of God moving and operating in the lives of his people that there would be times that I would have to confront some issues and some people. Now not only was this the case as a leader in the church but in the Navy as well. Now the Navy is a whole other ball game. There is no central moral code that we all live by and we don't all have the same belief, therefore, due to this fact, working with people who are from different places, who come from various backgrounds, experiences, and insight, there will almost always be confrontation. Though the two platforms of leadership are different and host two separate missions, beliefs, and environments, they both require the ability to confront and manage conflict. Through it all, as leaders confrontation is often looked at in a negative manner and a topic not easily discussed but here I want to discuss its advantages.

Yep, confrontation has its advantages and can have a major positive impact on the lives of those who are involved. Now how is this possible, because I've always heard that confrontation was stressful, awkward, and came with negative results. I've even witnessed how conflict separated friends, families, churches, and destroyed businesses. So how in the world am I confidently saying that confrontation can be majorly positive. Well here are a few reasons why:

#1 Identify Your Voice

There is nothing like winning your first basketball game, football game, picking up your first professional contract, or overcoming your fear of heights. You gain a sense of achievement, success, and confidence about yourself because you were able overcome, persevere, and see something through. Well, I challenge you to think about confrontation in that way. I was so afraid of confrontation that I didn't have a voice. I didn't know how to speak up, what to say, or even if people would listen to me, but when I started speaking up, I gained more confidence and I learned that people had been waiting for me to speak.

If you are a man reading this book, please take hold to this point. If you are one of my sisters, you can sit on this secret as well. Let's continue!

It's funny that as men, people especially our wives, standby to hear us speak. They love to hear us command, set order, and take control. They love to hear us speak in confidence and declare the word of God. Believe me when I tell you! They love to watch us as we do our thing, however, if we succumb to fear, we will never get that opportunity leaving those around us to wonder who we really are.

Bro, one of the most powerful things you possess is your words. Check out what the bible says about them in Proverbs 12: 6(NLT) says "The words of the wicked are like a murderous ambush, but the words of the godly save lives". Man look at this, this scripture tells us that the words of the godly saves lives. Therefore, if you are given the opportunity to confront someone, not only are you exposing their error, but you also have the opportunity to save them from their very own destruction. Imagine what would happen if God stopped telling you what you're doing wrong. Imagine who you would become if God decided to stop speaking to you. That would be crazy right? But that is the same way you should value your own words and understand that as a man, there are people who are living based off of what you say.

So believe me, your VOICE MATTERS and not only does your voice matter in the lives of those around you, your voice definitely matters to God and holds a lot of weight. I mean some heavy weight! John 15: 7(NLT) says, "But if you remain in me and my words remain in you, you may ask for anything you want, and it will be granted!" This is a great scripture, but check the relationship between our words and our relationship with God. If you have a pure relationship with God, the scripture says that you may ask for anything you want, and it will be granted. So if things aren't moving in your life, marriage, business, church, job, or community, it's probably because you're not saying the right things and have an unstable relationship with God.

If so, take some time to realign yourself with God and watch how your words bring about more blessings and opportunities than your works, talents, gifts, or skills can produce combined.

#2 Prevents Confusion

Recently I had the opportunity to meet with one of the brothers of my church about his lifestyle. Now he is one that is filled with much potential, drive, giftings, and anointing, but looking at his life you would never know. For years I stood by and watched him live in a cycle of inconsistency, doubt, and unproductivity, and now was the time to confront him. So myself and a few other leaders sat down and confronted him with the truth.

The bible tells us that the truth will set us free and that's what the power of confrontation can do. So we shared with him our observations and concerns and exposed him to what he couldn't see. This is one of the beauties of confrontation because many times, people are doing things that they are not aware of and it takes a strong person who isn't afraid of being attacked, to confront the person who may not perceive their own actions. However, after our session, he was able to see, acknowledge, and trace the things that we talked about and develop a plan of action to prevent those things from happening again.

This is a great nugget to take as a leader because it is your job to ensure that those who work for you or serve with you are producing their greatest efforts, if they aren't, you should be able to provide them insight on how to be better. There have been many instances in my life where I thought I was doing the right things but I wasn't. There were many other things that I thought I was doing at the right time and I wasn't, but because I had an amazing mother, leader, friends, family, and ultimately God, I was able to take the information and change my life if I chose too. So remember that, as a leader, It is not your job to take care of your people or run their entire lives, it is our duty to drop seeds of improvement hoping that they will take them on, and improve on their own. The more truthful you are with those around you, the less confusion can run their lives and the more they can live in clarity and walk in purpose. So keep on speaking!

#3 Gives insight to the Future

I've learned many times in the midst of facing confrontation that It's easy to focus on the moment. It's easy to focus on the assignment that was late, or the birthday that was missed, or the curfew that was not met, but another beauty of confrontation is that it gives you the ability to cast vision. Not only does it give you the ability to cast vision but it also gives you the ability to present hope. For example, speaking of the same brother I spoke about earlier in the chapter, we were able to share with him our vision for his life and where he could be in the future. We were able to show him that there was so much more to life than what he was experiencing and that he had the ability to reach it. I didn't understand this truth before but now I do.

The blessing in being confronted is that it exposes the wrong of one's past mistakes and can introduce the possibility of their future. A great leader will find a way to not only correct their team but simultaneously inspire them to be better and you have what it takes to do them both.

This is a great time to stop and think about how God stopped you in your tracks, confronted you, and simultaneously showed you the possibilities of your future with him. Corporately, when we get saved, God shows us that we no longer have to live a life of sin or be burdened down by destructive living. Actually the bible says it this way, "This means that anyone who belongs to Christ has become a new person. The old life is gone; a new life has begun" (2 Corinthians 5: 17, NLT). See this doesn't happen because all of a sudden we changed our minds and decided to be better. Nope, God comes into our lives, fights for us, cleans us up, and sends us on a new path of life partnered with his vision. I tell people all the time, I don't know when I stopped watching porn. I was addicted to it for years and watched it daily, but after I gave my life to Christ, he gave me new passions and confronted my old destructive ones.

Sometimes confronting people is hard, uncomfortable, and rather intimidating but reviewing the three beneficial effects of confrontation, don't you think it's worth it? As stated before, confronting conflict helps you to identify your voice, prevents confusion, and gives insight to one's future. Who would not want that? Who would not want their life to get a little easier, but let's be honest, it's not as easy to confront or be confronted. It's not easy to be told what's wrong or to tell someone their wrong. It's not easy to be exposed or to expose but again it's worth it for the possible increase that will come after it.

In all, fear is the ultimate enemy of confrontation and will keep you from being blessed and able to elevate in every area of your life. Though you may be talented, gifted, and knowledgeable, without the ability to confront others and even yourself, you won't be able to live the life that God has called you to live. Though this chapter dealt a lot on confronting others from the aspect of a leader, husband, brother, CEO, etc, I've found that confronting others is easier than confronting yourself. It can be somewhat of a scary process to confront yourself and acknowledge your own wrong but as I sit on this park bench at 9:30a.m , I've had to confront myself about how I have been treating the process of writing this book.

Writing this book is not only a personal accomplishment but there are those around me who can benefit from it as well. There are men all over the world who can benefit from it and the more I procrastinate and walk in complacency, the ones who need this book won't be able to use it to change their lives.

By you reading this book right now means that I was able to defeat procrastination and get the book published. By you reading this proves that I was able to confront myself and grow from it. So I end with this question:

What about you do you need to confront in order to enhance your life and the lives of others? Once you are able to answer this question, watch how your life and the lives of those around you go to another level of production . I love you and God Bless! I'll see you in the next chapter.

ROBERT B. VANN

CHAPTER 3
I'M A LOVER AND A FIGHTER

1 Samuel 17:45

David replied to the Philistine, "You come to me with sword, spear, and javelin, but I come to you in the name of the Lord of Heaven's Armies- the God of the armies of Israel, whom you have defied.

Have you heard the phrase "I'm a lover, not a fighter?" What comes to mind when hearing this phrase? I've said it on multiple occasions - when saying it, I was implying that loving is more important than fighting. However, I've come to realize that there are certain times when fighting is necessary. For the sake of clarity, I am not promoting physical violence, the fighting that I'm talking about is more mental, emotional, and spiritual. Unfortunately, as men, most of us are taught to fight physically to solve our problems or to prove our manhood; we are rarely taught how to submit to God and allow him to fight our battles. I have struggled with the aforementioned mindset for a long time; therefore, in this chapter, I'm going to share with you a few ways to be a lover and a fighter while using strategizes to fight for yourself, family, marriage, church, and your community. Let's get it!

Do you Have my Back?

When I was about 12 years old, I remember being on the bus one morning heading to school and my homeboy Ashton asked me if I would have his back if he were to get in a fight later that day and I said yes. Now let me be honest, though I said yes, I was terrified. I had never been in a fight before, but for my homie, I was willing to figure it out even if it costs me getting my butt whooped. Needless to say, I didn't have to fight that day or any other day for that matter.

Out of my 28 years of life, I've never been in a physical altercation with another person. I know, I know, how in the heck is that possible. How is it possible for a man to avoid having at least one neighborhood or schoolyard brawl? Well, don't judge me and stay focused, but know that this sets the tone for the rest of the chapter because there were a couple of reasons that I had not fought. First of all, I never learned how to fight. Secondly, I was afraid of confrontation; lastly, I've always been a pretty cool-headed guy who made friends with everyone which latter hindered me as a man.

Have you ever been in a situation where you had to stand up for somebody? How did it make you feel? What led you to stand up for them? What did you do? I start with these questions because there're many times that we're able to stand up for others, but we're reluctant to stand up for ourselves. If you are like who I was, you may not know how to stand up for yourself. If I were to go a bit deeper in this point, you might not see a reason to stand up or to fight for yourself. This was the root of my lack of ferocity and drive because I failed to see my worth, value, or reason for being. This mentality is what caused me not to be able to stand up for myself on multiple occasions. Therefore, knowing who you are and whose you are is the first step of being a lover and a fighter and will help you to determine those that you're supposed to fight for as well.

You are not your Mistakes

Have you ever felt that you were your worst critic? Every time you make a mistake, forget something or fail to meet an accomplishment, you beat yourself up and condemn yourself for failing. Now you may not always say this out loud

YOU ARE A STRONG MAN

or even to others, but subconsciously every time you make a mistake you begin to withdraw from others internally and work harder to please them to prevent them from seeing your flaws. I've done this for years and have witnessed the debilitating effects of these efforts. I thought doing more for people would help boost my self-esteem and improve their perspectives of me, but It didn't and made me feel worse. Therefore, because of this, when I needed to speak up for myself, I couldn't. When I needed to stand up for what I believed I couldn't. I would rather compromise my beliefs, standards, and morals to be friendly and prevent conflict rather than to stand up for myself and to fight for what was right.

Let me remind you of David, the son of Jesse in 1 Samuel chapter 16 and 17 who was a young shepherd boy in charge of tending to his father's sheep. David was the youngest out of seven (7) older brothers in which three (3) of them are described as warriors who fought for the Israelite Army. These chapters lay out a story of David's life that is critical to your own because it teaches how love will make you fight and how to identify the tools you could use to defeat your enemy. For this chapter's sake, the enemy could be several things such as the devil, your past, pain, mentality, or a threat to your family, churches, or community's welfare. So, keep an open mind and allow God to reveal to you what enemies you are to defeat.

Now if you read the story, you will see that Jesse, David's father, sent him to take some food to his brothers who were out on the battlefield. When David arrived, he was amazed at what he saw because there was a great giant there taunting the army of God, and the soldiers were stricken with fear and unable to defend themselves. Witnessing this, David began to ask questions inquiring about the reward for the one who would defeat the giant. Though this was a noble and courageous gesture, his brother Eliab was upset. He was so angry that he antagonized David and disrespectfully took a shot at David's job as a shepherd, but David didn't respond. David went on to speak to King Saul and received his blessing to fight the battle against the opposing giant and would do it courageously.

Understanding this story perfectly provides the framework upon which I will base the rest of this chapter and teach how love will make you fight even if you don't believe you can or have the tools to be successful. First off, let me remind you that David wasn't a fighter or trained to war in battle, he was classified as a shepherd just like some of us who may not look like a warrior, but we are within. You may not be a preacher, pastor, chief executive officer (C.E.O), Business Owner, Executive director, or community activist, but there is a battle for you to fight. I truly believe that every man has a battle that God has specifically designed them to fight. Whether your battle is mentoring youth, leading churches, or ministering to incarcerated young men, there is a good-fight for you. Goliath looks different to everyone and the tools we use to win the VICTORY differ as well; therefore, don't be discouraged if your giant doesn't look as important as others or your weapons of war don't look as effective; KEEP ON FIGHTING.

Now back to David; though David was a shepherd and in charge of tending to his father's sheep, he had experience in fighting his own battles. As a shepherd when a lion or bear threatened David's sheep, he was responsible for defeating every threat that came their way, and he did. I share this with you because though you may not have defeated the giant of global poverty or found the cure for cancer; you have defeated the giant of suicide and hopelessness. As a husband, working as hard as you can to provide for your wife and children, you have defeated the giant of fatherless homes that plagues the landscape of our society. Even if you aren't living with your children; you are still trying to take care of them and your part as a father. Because of this, I want you to take pride in the little battles that you've won because as you do that, you will gain the confidence necessary to face the bigger giants to come.

If David didn't love the sheep, he wouldn't have protected them. If he didn't care for them, he would've let them die. So, when it came to defeating the giant to ensure that his brothers and family would live, he was willing to step up and fight because he had experience in winning small battles.

Love has been known to make people do some crazy things as well as some good things. For example, love can make an acholic put the bottle down and start drinking water or love can make a person erase all the female contacts in their phone except their girlfriend's. Love will make a man get off the couch and get a job or get out of the bed and go to the gym. Shoot, love will make you drop the side-chick and become a faithful man! Most importantly, love will make you drop your agenda and give your life to God like Peter did by the sea of Galilee. Because love was so powerful to David, he didn't allow his status to hinder him from saving lives and doing what he knew was right.

David loved his people so much that he was willing to put himself in harm's way to save their lives. I present this point because most of the time as men, we often feel like we are putting our lives at risks for everybody else. It seems like it's only our responsibility to provide. It's our responsibility to protect. It's our responsibility to lead, and if you're like me these things can be tiresome. These things can become a burden, and though we love the ones who benefit from our strength, we're slowly dying internally. So, while you are ensuring that everybody else around you is happy, fed, and taken care of, start using that effort to take care of yourself as well.

Fight for Yourself

Growing up, for a very long time, I felt that my mother didn't fight for me and that my father didn't either when him and my mother separated. Because of this, from an early age, I began to live a life of insecurity and defeat. I was angry with them because I felt that they should've done a better job of managing their lives for the sake of me. (How selfish did I sound?). I thought that no one was looking out for what I wanted or needed in life. I was afraid, and many days even as a 28-year-old man, I still felt that way. These menacing thoughts tormented me for so long that I didn't know how to stick up for myself. I didn't understand what to say when I was offended, and I was afraid of the backlash if I did. I was trapped in a prison of fear that I created and blamed others for my instability. However, God has shown me my worth and value, but if I'm honest, I'm finally at a point in my life that I'm ready to live my best life.

Have you ever known that there was more to your life than what was currently there and it frustrated you to the point that you had no choice but to change? Well that's where I am right now. Going through a divorce has truly opened my eyes. Within the last year, my wife moved out and into a separate apartment twice. During this time we've spoken, and she said that I'm an amazing husband. Confused? Yeah, I know because sitting and listening to her speak those words while desiring to leave put me in bad place. How could I be a great husband, but my wife not want to be with me? How could I be a great husband, but my wife was moving out again? It was at that moment I realized I'd lost a sense of me! I lost my purpose and love for self. It was so bad that I would look to others to show me why I was worth being loved. My self-esteem was so low that God couldn't even change my mind; however, He blessed me with this trial and opened my eyes to the truth.

Strategies to Protect You

This chapter is devoted to you. Not how you can fight for your wife, children, or strategies to protect your home, church, or community. What I'm learning is that men need to learn how to fight for themselves first, and when they have mastered that, they will naturally protect everything that is around them. So how can you protect or fight for you? This chapter we're going to focus on protecting your emotional, spiritual, and physical well-being. I know this may not be what you were expecting, but anyone of these areas can drastically affect your life and those around you, so let's take a look at each one of them at a time:

Emotional Well-Being

Your emotional state is very important and lines up with your physical and your spiritual wellbeing. The bible even talks about this by saying, "Guard your heart above all else, for it determines the course of your life" (Proverbs 14: 23, NLT). Then the bible goes on to say, "O my son, give me your heart. May your eyes take delight in following my ways" (Proverbs 23: 26). Though these scriptures are different, they work in conjunction with each other and the context upon which to build our strategy towards how to protect our emotions. Though emotions are simply feelings, those feelings are interpreted to come from our hearts, but they are essentially recognized, internalized, and analyzed through the receptors of your minds.

As the scripture says, guard your heart above all else. As men, we must be protective of who and what we are giving our hearts too. I know we like to say that we are hard, rugged, and try to act like we don't have feelings sometimes, but if we are not careful, we will mishandle the thing that gives us life and put it into the hands of something or someone that will destroy it. Look at those who repeatedly give their hearts to a woman who mistreats them, bosses who disregard them, family members who disvalue them, or even things like drugs, alcohol, porn, fear, anxiety, stress, and shame. We must understand that the heart is the most important organ in the body because it is the instrument that supplies and pumps all the life-giving blood to and throughout our entire bodies; therefore, we can't just treat it any way we want to, we must value it.

The heart is so powerful that most men are afraid to use it or deny even having one. It brings us so much fear to love sometimes that we would rather destroy the opportunity of being loved or loving someone because we are afraid of being emotional or being hurt by someone that we were emotionally connected too. A lot of men also struggle with being emotional, not because they don't want to be, but because they were trained not to be. They were trained that emotionalism is weakness and that real men don't show weakness or cry. Former generations of men prided themselves on being strong, rugged, and hard workers while lacking the emotional capability to be loving and compassionate towards their children or spouses. This type of man was completely fine with bringing home the bacon but was not fine with sitting down and cuddling with his son, daughter, or spouse. Emotionally they were cutoff and insensitive for various reasons, but I'm praying that you will rise above these hurdles and be open to love and receive love as God has designed you too.

So, the main way to protect your heart is to give it to God. Well, how is that done? I'm glad you asked: To start, you must decide to trust God and love him daily. Every day you wake up, you must choose to follow His lead and allow his love to sweep you off your feet. You must open yourself up to him and worship him as your savior and your God. Giving your heart to Him is simply confessing that he is your Lord, Savior, and friend and that you will serve him as best as you can even as you make mistakes. Give him your life by putting his desires before your own and ensure that you keep him first and above all others.

Now, this is not going to be easy because you're going to be confronted daily with challenges, distractions, temptations, and setbacks, but even in those moments, confess Him to be God and trust him no matter what. Fight for your heart and protect it because you are worth it but don't be so overprotective that you push people away.

Spiritual Well-Being

Beyond the importance of your emotions, your spirit is the most important. As men of God, we must continue to strengthen our spirit because in us lies no good thing. Our natural desires are perverted, selfish, and sinful; therefore, we must protect our spirit daily. We can do this by reading the word of God, fasting, praying, praising, and worshipping God. See our spirit is like a muscle, the more you work it, the stronger it gets. Look at Ephesians 6: 10(NLT) which says, "A final word: Be strong in the Lord and in his mighty power." Then 1 Corinthians 16: 13-14(NLT) says, "Be on guard. Stand firm in the faith. Be courageous. Be Strong. And do everything with love." You have to put these scriptures into your database because they provide the foundations upon which every strong man shall stand.

Look at Ephesians 6: 10(NLT) again, which says, "A final word: Be strong in the Lord and in his mighty power." This is important to you because it carries a theme that you don't have to be strong on your own. It shows us that we can live through the strength of God and allow his power to flow through us. Then 1 Corinthians 16: 13- 14(NLT), gives us a few directions on what strength looks like practically by telling us to be on guard, firm in the faith, courageous, strong, and to walk in love. These are the five (5) attributes of a Strong man, but they can only truly be demonstrated when that man is spiritually healthy. Therefore, be watchful in all that you do, seek God daily and get to know his voice because there are spiritual forces that desire to take you out and distract you from being the Strong Man that God has called you to be. Let's look at one example.

Simon Peter was a devoted disciple of Jesus Christ. He was kind of hot-headed and was not afraid to speak his mind, but there came a time in his life that he would be tested beyond measure. Jesus prepares him for this test by saying the following words, "Simon, Simon, Satan has asked to sift each of you like wheat. But I have pleaded in prayer for you, Simon, that your faith should not fail. So, when you have repented and turned to me again, strengthen your brothers." Looking over this scripture, do you see how great of a God Jesus is?

Do you see the all-knowing power of our God that is able to warn us of a battle before we get into it, then be able to assure us that we won't lose while we are in it? Not only did Jesus say that Simon would turn to Him again, but that when he is strengthened, he will strengthen his brothers. In summary, this is the whole point of this book. Spiritually, I was weak, bruised, battered, hurt, tired, and needed help; but God didn't let me die in the process, he covered me, and as I turned to him, he strengthened me and gave me the vision to strengthen my brothers. The strength did not come from the outside; it came from the inside.

Remember, earlier in this chapter I said that some men aren't able to fight for others because they can't fight for themselves - well, that was me. I finally gave up pleasing people, being afraid of others, and other things just so I could get in the face of God and worship him. The result of this choice is in your hands right now via paperback, hardcopy, e-book, or audiobook. This book is not another self-help book for me; it's way more than that. This is my turn experience. This is a gift to men and women all over the world who are in the midst of a turn. You're not quite who you were, but you aren't where you're going. You're in the midst of a turn. However, the speed of your turn is determined by how fast you understand, repent, and turn again to serve and worship God with all your heart, soul, and mind.

Physical Well-Being

In an article titled Signs and Symptoms of Heart Disease in Men, authors Robin Donovan and Kristeen Cherney write about heart health as it pertains to men and it is truly eye-opening. They open up their article by saying, "Heart disease is one of the leading health risks facing men today. According to the American Heart Association (AHA), more than one in three adult men has heart disease. Heart disease is an umbrella term that includes: heart failure, coronary artery disease, arrhythmias, angina, other heart-related infections, irregularities, and birth defects" (https://www.healthline.com/health/heart-disease/signs-men, 2017).

The authors further state that, "Many men are at high risk of developing heart disease. The AHA reported in 2013 that only a quarter of men met federal guidelines for physical activity in 2011. They also estimated that 72.9 percent of U.S. men age 20 and older are overweight or obese. And about 20 percent of men smoke, which can cause the blood vessels to narrow. Narrowed blood vessels are a precursor to certain types of heart disease" (2017).

Scary but true, men are at a higher risk for heart disease than anyone else and the rate for heart disease increases for African American men and other minorities. Therefore, we have to take care of ourselves. I know we enjoy an occasional beer, wine, cigar, cigarette, fast-food, or doughnut, but is it all worth your life? I, for one, experienced my first episode of heart problems back in 2018. I went into the Navy Medical clinic for a routine check-up, and they end up finding an irregularity in my heartbeat. The doctor said that my blood pressure was high and that I was having heart palpitations. They sent me off and made me come back three consecutive times to monitor and track the trend of my blood pressure levels. On one of my visits, they decided to recheck my heart and found that the heart palpitations were continuing and rushed me off to the Virginia Beach emergency room in an ambulance.

This was an eye-opening experience and exposed me to the realities of life and how easy I could lose it. After further tests and evaluations, doctors discovered the root of my heart problems by asking one simple "Sir, have you been stressed out about anything lately?" I responded with, "Yes sir, I am currently going through a divorce." Unbeknownst to me, it wasn't the food that I was eating that was destroying my heart, it was the stress that I was fostering that was eating me up from the inside out. The doctor went on to say that stress is indeed a silent killer and that if you're not careful, stress will take you out without anyone knowing what happened. Therefore, if you are under any amount of stress, please seek professional help, counseling, therapy, or medical attention, because you may be on the verge of a heart attack or stroke and you wouldn't even know it.

I don't know what you've been through, who may have left, rejected, or abandoned you but know today that you're somebody. I don't care what you've done, haven't done, said, or haven't said, you're a King! The bible tells us that we're a royal priesthood, a peculiar people, a holy nation, and a chosen generation, and that isn't based on our acts, that's based off God's love. He knew you would mess up, He knew you would make mistakes, He knew you would hurt people, but He died for you to ask Him for forgiveness and to live again. God had to come to earth because the Mosaic law didn't have any room for grace or mercy; therefore, for us to be forgiven for our sins, we have to go to Christ. So, I'm telling you today that you're a King!

You're a man and don't give up on yourself. Pick your head up! Go before God and worship, allow Him to restore your joy, peace, and strength and walk in

His ordained purpose for your life because your tomorrow shall be greater than your yesterday. Fight King Fight! You are worth it, and I declare that as you learn how to fight for yourself, you will gain the strength and the strategies necessary to fight for others. Keep on fighting Strong Man, because the Lord is fighting for you.

CHAPTER 4
SEX: DO YOU SEE ME

"Your sexual performance should not be used as a business card to display your services. Sex was created by God in order for a Husband and a wife to serve each other."

-Robert B. Vann

I wonder if she even notices me?" This is a question that haunted me during years of my marriage. I knew we were married, living in the same house, and loved each other but I often felt like we were roommates instead of spouses and associates instead of best friends. This is an unfortunate truth because it caused me to become very insecure about the condition of our marriage. So, the only way I knew to balance out my value in my marriage was sex. Sex was the thermometer I used to measure her love, attraction, and desire towards me on various occasions. This is not because I always wanted to have sex or even had the urge too, usually it was a means to get her attention. I know this is crazy for a man to admit but maybe you have found yourself using or have used sex as a tool to measure your masculinity or ensuring that you are noticed by someone. If so, I want to discuss how the means of using sex to validate our manhood, enhance our self-esteem, and determine our value is dangerous and unhealthy to our self-esteem and teach us how to value and validate ourselves in a positive way.

Bro, Be Honest!

Have you ever had sex with someone then wondered why you did it? Or on a deeper level, even wondered why you chose the one you had sex with? When you look at yourself and the person you chose to have sex with, you wondered, "WHAT WAS I THINKING?" Bro, you probably wouldn't even tell you homeboys about her because you knew they wouldn't approve of her. Well, I did this plenty of times and till this day wonder, Robert, what the heck was wrong with you, lol. See, I know growing up sex was popularized and plastered over TV, social media, and other marketing platforms as a romantic/exotic moment of passion between two lovers and often strangers who were intensely attracted to each other. However, as much as I tried to recreate those cinematic moments, I could never achieve what I saw, and I wonder why?

Societies view on Men and Sex

"From countless teen movies to comments on online forums, the adult virgin male is branded as a bit of a loser. While female virginity may still retain some virtue in modern western society, male virginity certainly does not" says writer Harry Siva, author of the article Is the Adult Male Virgin Society's Last Taboo? Speaking about the view of social status of men and our sexual habits, Siva later writes, "Indeed, the logic and vernacular of professional pick-up artists (PUAs) suggest that men who bed multiple women "demonstrate higher value." They're the sought-after "alpha males" with something to offer society. They have high social status. Reasoned this way, the adult man who has not even slept with one woman, let alone multiple women, is the "beta male". He has low social status. He is a male of little value." With these facts being surprising but strikingly true, how are we as men supposed to validate ourselves outside of our sexual performance?

Especially as men of faith, whether you are married or not, how are we supposed to place value on ourselves if our sexual performance is supposedly our only measuring tool? Bro, it is hard out here! I'm newly divorced, after being married for 7 years, and I must work hard every day not to react impulsively to my sexual desires. Yeah, I love God, worship, and adore him, but Lord Jesus, there are truly some beautiful women in this world. I'm not even stressing about sex for real, but being new to singleness, it is hard not to acknowledge every beautiful woman that crosses my path. Throughout the rest of this chapter, I am going to share with you my experience with sex and the trap it placed me in as a single/non-married, and how that same prison followed me into my marriage.

Holding out for Marriage

Whether you have been raised in church or not, you probably have heard of the term, "I'm Saving myself for marriage." You hear it a lot from our female counterparts but you rarely, if at all, hear it from men. Well, I didn't quite make this vow to myself or to God but now I wish I would've because the torment and constant flashes of past experiences haunt me to this day. Let me tell you how this all got started. So, like many of my friends growing up, every one of us was after girls and Oh what a joy it was. We found pride in ourselves on the amount of numbers we could attain, the content of our conversations, and the results of those conversations. The social climate basically commanded you to have sex or at least seem like you were, and that was my angle. So, all throughout high school I talked a good talk. You would think that I was an experienced movie star by the way I was able to talk about my fake experiences in the bedroom but to be honest, I was terrified. I was scared, inexperienced, and knew that it was wrong.

See, growing up in church, I knew what was right and wrong but doing the right thing was not popular and that's even the case now. So, after being a virgin for 18 years, I gave in. It was the best and worst 30 seconds ever and would send me on a journey that I was not ready for. Between the ages of 18 and 21, I would come to have sex with many women, protected and not protected sex. I was having so much fun and no longer had to brag about my fake experiences, I was finally a man. I was confident and had a few notches on my belt. You couldn't tell me nothing. Girl after girl, I would conquer and then move to another while setting up the next one and this cycle went on for a while until It didn't. Something was different. At first, the experience of the moment was exciting and fulfilling, but my actions would later become more draining. I didn't quite understand it back then, but sex was starting to hurt me internally. I was too afraid to confront that truth so I covered it up by having more sex hoping that my feelings towards it would eventually change but It didn't.

I share my story with you because on the surface, I was just doing what boys do. On the surface I was just figuring out my body and expressing my sexuality, but the truth was that I was hurting and using those girls as a means of escape from my life. The truth is, I wasn't happy. Though I lived in a home where I never had to worry about food, lights, or clothing; though I was excelling in school, active in church, and a part of many extracurricular activities. After having sex with a girl, I would literally be upset with myself because of what I did and who I did it with. The truth is, I wanted to be loved, I wanted to be held, I wanted to feel secure, I wanted someone to wrap me in their arms and say that they loved me.

There was a void missing in my life as a young man and I was searching for it in any woman that would give me attention. I didn't care what she looked like, all I wanted to know is if she was willing to spend time with me. I was not happy, and though I am talking about my childhood, I believe many men are feeling that way right now. We have families, heading up companies, faithful to our Churches, serving our communities, and many other things but we aren't happy. So, the closest and easiest thing to do is to utilize our bodies to validate our worth.

God's View on Sex

We may not admit it, but men want to be loved too! We desire it with a passion! We deeply want to have a connection with someone who will care for us. We deeply want someone who is devoted to the cares of our hearts, but when we don't receive that, we result to what's common to us, and for most of us that is sex. I say sex, because sex is the closest relationship and connection that humans can have with each other. Therefore, God deemed it as sacred and holds sex at such a high regard because when a man and woman join, they are mirroring the relationship that the triune share. They become one, therefore, our bodies are sacred in God's eyes and should be treated with the utmost respect. 1 Corinthians 6: 19 echoes this point by saying, "Don't you realize that your body is the temple of the Holy Spirit, who lives in you and was given to you by God? You do not belong to yourself," (NLT). I believe this scripture draws out two important points that we as men need to know.

First, this scripture points out that our bodies are the temple or housing place for the Holy Spirit to live. This is important to know as it pertains to sex because God can't live in a defiled or unclean temple and when we are having sex outside of marriage, that makes our bodies unclean. As men of God, this truth we must digest because for us to live the life that God wants us to live, we must have him active in our lives daily. We need him to live and be present on the inside of us so that we can access his power, fruit, and gifts that bring us in line with his plan for our lives.

Without the Holy Spirit living in us we are lifeless and left to live under the leadership of our flesh instead of the governance of God's Spirit and we don't want that.

Secondly, the scriptures reveal to us that we are not our own, we belong to God. This truth also acknowledges that all rights to us, our bodies, and our soul belongs to God; what we do with them is up to us. Writer of 1 Corinthians 3: 17 gives his readers insight on how God deals with those who mistreat their bodies and that of others by saying, "God will destroy anyone who destroys this temple. For God's temple is holy, and you are that temple." (NLT). This may seem a bit harsh, but you must understand why this is so.

God created our total being in the Image and Likeness of himself. He created us out of the dirt of the ground and blew into our nostrils the breath of life and we became living souls. God hand crafted and covered us in our mother's womb only to reveal us to the earth as representatives of the kingdom of God. Therefore, by destroying and devaluing our bodies through careless acts of sex we taint God's image and prevent him from displaying his face in the earth. Now you don't want to be one that hinders God's ability to reach his people on earth, do you? I ask this because Psalms 115: 16 says, "The heavens belong to the Lord, but he has given the earth to all humanity." (NLT). See in the bible we see a transition of power. God initially gave the authority to govern and rule the earth to man then man messed up, so God sent Jesus. Once Jesus came down to earth then ascended back to heaven, he left the Holy Spirit in his place to dwell in man and to be active on earth. Therefore, God gets access to earth by the power of the Holy Spirit and through the obedience of his children which cannot take place if we defile our bodies due to sexual immorality. So, why do we do it?

Well the bible says that we are wrapped in sin and shaped in iniquity so there is a natural desire for us to be sinful and walk in perversion. Not only that, but we must fight against the spiritual forces of darkness that strive daily to persuade us to perform evil acts outside of the will of God. Though these two points are true, I've discovered that one of the most powerful motivators for sex is a void of love due to abandonment or rejection. There is nothing worse than feeling unwanted by someone who is supposed to want you. It is the craziest thing to have a father but feel that they don't love you, a mother that never nurtures you, or a wife who pay's you no attention. Scenarios like this that takes place in a man's life can have various effects on him and his self-esteem and how he reacts to this type of environment can vary.

Having my own abandonment and rejection issues with my father at an early age, I resulted to the first thing I knew that could replace what I felt that he was supposed to give. I'm not blaming my father for my ways; I'm just explain my pathology in case you may have faced what I have or have a son that could be experiencing the same thing. So, because I was lacking the love from my father, I looked to porn and sex to replace him. It was like I was using every woman to prove that I existed! Have you ever felt that you were alive but didn't exist? Like, you are physically alive, going to work, picking up the kids, and taking the trash out but during your responsibilities you don't feel alive or relevant? This was my way of thinking. I knew I was physically alive, but I didn't feel important enough to be relevant. So, in my marriage, for me, sex became a means of validating my existence instead of a shared experience of pleasure. It got so bad that I desired to have sex more than I desired to be in the presence of God because I believed that having sex was a greater source of love than worshipping God. I would literally think about it all day but then be afraid to ask.

Yes, you read right. I would desire sex so bad, but I would be so afraid to ask. How is that possible? I would be so terrified to ask that I would tremble and literally close my eyes after I pressed send on a text message talking about sex. I was afraid to be rejected and the truth is I was surprised that she said yes. As a side note: I've learned that many people would rather choose to watch porn rather than to have sex with the opposite sex in order to prevent themselves from being rejected by them. However, I was broken, confused, hurt, afraid, and unsure. I knew I could work hard, cut the grass, wash the dishes, wash the cars, and fold clothes but those things didn't validate my manhood. In my mind, the only thing that validated my manhood was sex.

Come on man think about it. What do you and your friends talk about after one of your birthdays or anniversaries? The first thing we want to know is if you got some. If we did, we get so excited and love to talk about it but if we don't, we're nowhere near as excited and we're hoping that the day after will be better. It's like sex has become the badge of manhood that allows us into the National I'm a Man Club, so if one was a virgin or not as "experienced" as another they are not qualified to join the club. Well I'm telling you today, that God created you in the image of himself, therefore, you were a man before you were even born, and sex doesn't define who you are.

Where are My Single Kings At?

Let me tell you something bro, I have been single for a few months now and it is REAL! I honor you if you have been single for a day, a few months, or even a few years. Bro, I don't see how you are making it, LOL. As I stated earlier, I am a man of God, who loves him dearly, but there are times when a brotha just wants to be held. Just last week, I recognized that as my confidence grows as a single man, my desire to be with woman grows. It's weird, because as I grow to love myself more, I desire to show someone how great I am. Not in an arrogant way, but in a posture that recognizes that I finally see myself as valuable and believe that I am ready to take on the challenge of a true relationship. However, I quickly digress because I understand that I have a little more work to do, but whenever I find my good thing, she is going to be blessed and have a King at her side.

I'm taking the time in this chapter to write to you to encourage you to keep pressing and to say that I understand. To be honest, I used to judge single men, especially single male Christians because I thought they were weak and constantly back sliding. From my married perspective, those single men didn't have the faith to walk in purity and control their desires, but boy was I wrong. Now it's different if I was single and didn't have much going for myself and was a dead beat, but when the ladies see a good man, they come after it. Now tell me I'm not telling the truth. How many times have you caught a sister at your church, job, school, etc. giving you the side eye? Giving you that "Boy he just doesn't know" look! Come on bro, don't leave me hanging.

One thing I know about God is that when he saves a man and cleans him up, no matter who he was before, he changes him and gives him an edge. It's like a new confidence comes over us and our walk changes. Our talk changes and the way we view ourselves changes. Now this is only for those men who have decided to truly give their lives to God, but for those who do, he gives us what I like to call, "God Swag"! God swag consists of group of tools that God gives a man when he decides to give his life to God. These tools include but aren't limited too: A vision, plan, anointing, new perspective, humility, servants' heart, boldness, clarity, confidence, and a desire for greater good for all mankind. Now if you have a few of these but are missing one or a few, it's okay because God releases them at different times, but when he does, you will see your life change dramatically and others will notice.

Therefore, to my single brother, I need to you to be careful about getting big headed about your newfound swag because there will be many women who admire you for it. I've found this to be true, because though I am not perfect, I got the God Swag! I'm a man of vision, integrity, love, anointing, and service and many women would love to have a man like me. However, though this is true, there are some who are attracted to me, not because of who I am, but because of who God has anointed me to be. They don't necessarily know me, my weirdness, pet peeves, bloopers, and struggles, they're attracted to the God in me. I share this with you because if you're not on guard, you will end up getting into relationships and having sex with women that won't stay with you because once they found out who you really were outside of the anointing, they were no longer attracted. So, what am I saying bro, I know singleness is hard, but still, wait and let God cultivate you into the man he desires you to be and let him lead you to your wife in his timing. You will be thankful if you do!

To My Married Brothers!!

A while back I thought about teaching a class titled, "I might, I do, or I did"! This class was going to teach and encourage single men and married men on how to prepare and have successful sustainable marriages. Well that class never came to fruition, but I want to address its foundation in this chapter because there are truly some important things to discuss. The same way I expressed the difficulties of a single man, I believe it is even more difficult to be a successful and faithful husband. Listen, not only does God also provide a married Man with God Swag, but that married man must pivot all his God Swag efforts towards one woman. I don't care how holy you are, when you are a man with God Swag, you must make the decision every morning to focus solely on your wife and nobody else. Believe me, I know.

As a married man, there are many commands that God gives you concerning your body and sex within the confines of your marriage. The marriage bed is considered, undefiled, which is amiantos in the Greek which means free from that by which the nature of a thing is deformed or debased. Simply, Merriam Webster's dictionary defines it this way: not corrupt, impure, or unclean. Check out the scripture in which it is used: Hebrews 13: 4 says, "Marriage is honorable in all, and the bed undefiled: but whoremongers and adulterers God will judge" (KJV). In this scripture, God acknowledges that marriage is honorable, great, and amazing, but the bed is a place of purity, freedom, tenderness. Sex within the confines of marriage is untamed, free, explosive, and organic. It's supposed to be the purest and closest form to love and worship that a man and a woman can ever get to. However, there are times when sex within marriage can seem more agonizing and more of a burden than good.

Unfortunately, there are many married couples and even Christian couples who are going weeks, months, and even years without having sex. Either the man is no longer interested in his wife or the wife is uninterested in her husband, or the love that they once shared is so far gone that the fire that they once had for each other has gone out. It's sad to say that more often than one would think, there are many people around you today who share in this testimony and out of this comes thoughts of loneliness, rejection, and despair. Even as men who pride ourselves on being Alphas and desired by women, when we don't feel needed, we are hurt, shamed, and even embarrassed, I know I did! It's not easy to go to work, school, or class and to feel seen by people on the outside but not at home. It's not easy to work hard then to come home with no passion, later to go to work and to enjoy the smile of someone else.

If you have experienced this or are experiencing this right now, please, know that you are not alone. There are many men all over the world who are struggling with this same battle. There are many men who don't feel seen by their wives, girlfriends, children, etc. and are hurt and don't know what to do. Right now, if you are dealing with not feeling seen, wanted, desired, attractive, or are losing hope in yourself or marriage. Take this time to ask God to help you. Take this time to ask God to give you the strength to stay strong, give you the strength to love him, yourself, and your wife. Give you the strength to stay faithful and not give up on your marriage. Ask God to revive your love and to restore the fire in your marriage. Seek him daily and continue to show the love of God to your spouse until things turn around knowing that no matter what, God is with you, he loves you, cares about you and understands.

I was in this position while I was married. I was feeling unstable at home, unwanted, unloved, not seen and would leave and go out into the world everyday empty. I would go to work and go to class and see beautiful women. I would talk to them leisurely and innocently, without a deceitful motive or desire to get anything from them but after a while things started to change. I noticed that I liked the attention that I was getting. I liked being greeted with a smile when I got to work or being asked about what new business idea I was working on. I liked being able to joke freely and not have to think about being too silly or over the top. I liked being able to let my hair down and just chill. The truth is, I simply liked just being able to be me. After a while it got overwhelming, so I talked to my Pastor about it and stayed before God. The crazy thing was, no woman ever truly tried to make an advance at me while I was married but once, and when she did, I laughed it off. However, I didn't realize that just by getting attention from women that were not my wife was causing me to get weaker and weaker. Thank God, I didn't succumb to adultery physically, but I see now how emotionally I was tied to the idea of being wanted because I didn't feel wanted at home.

I wish I could blame this all on my ex-wife, but I can't because I could have communicated how I felt a long time ago. I could've expressed my voids and issues but as a man, I chose to hold it all in and handle it myself. What this did was isolate me to fix a problem that I could've never fix and kept her out of the loop of what was going on in my heart. Therefore, if you are married and are during this, no matter what stage of it you may be experiencing, tell your wife. I don't care how uncomfortable it may feel, scared you may be, or how she may react. Trust me, tell your wife! Don't try to fight off this temptation on your own, because it's only going to lead to a bad place if you do. You must give you wife the chance to change or assist you, that's why she is your help meet. Give her the chance to help you! See, all I had to do was be honest and say that I'm feeling unloved, unseen, unappreciated, and unattractive. As emasculating as that may seem, at least it would've given her the change to build me up.

I share my story with you to let you know that the devil only wants to divide and conquer. He only wants to separate you from your wife in order to get you two both in a corner without any assistance from your partner. This is because he knows that if he can separate you all, he can defeat you all. I wasn't able to close that gap in my marriage which ended in a divorce, but if you are married you still have a chance, and adultery or infidelity doesn't have to be your end. You don't have to cheat on your spouse. You don't have to have dm's full of mystery chicks, or a side chick on the side. Your marriage can thrive and so can your sex life, but you must want it too. Please understand, I'm showing God that I'm willing to save other marriages and relationships even though my ended the way it did. Actually, I needed it too. It made me stronger, tougher, wiser, more humble, and understanding to who God is, who I am, and how to appreciate others so please take heed and take the time you need to seek him, professional help, or surround yourself with good friends who will hold you accountable.

So, I'm telling you right now, you are valuable and necessary in the earth today. You don't have to wait until your next opportunity to have sex to feel like a strong man. You are a strong man because God said you are. You are a good man because God said you are, and the steps of a Good man are ordered by the Lord. There is no other greater love than that of Jesus Christ. No matter who has walked out on you or chosen someone instead of you. You are special, necessary, and relevant.

You don't have to auction off your body like a high-priced item, you are God's chosen Son and you shall do great things. The bible says that you were created in Jesus to do good works and that's exactly what you shall do. I declare right now that you shall walk in the confidence of God and be filled with the love of God right now in the Name of Jesus. You shall love the Lord your God with all your might, soul, and spirit, then love your neighbor as you love yourself. Your body is more important than what it can do for other people and your value is higher than the amount of sex you can have. There is no other love Greater than Jesus and you can receive his love today to fill the voids in your life in order for you to live happily and walk in the image that God has called you to walk in. You ARE a Strong Man, so walk in his Strength Today. Love ya Man!

CHAPTER 5
PORN: MY WAY OF ESCAPE!

1 Corinthians 6: 18-20(NLT)

18 Run from sexual sin! No other sin so clearly affects the body as this one does. For sexual immorality is a sin against your own body. 19 Don't you realize that your body is the temple of the Holy Spirit, who lives in you and was given to you by God? You do not belong to yourself, 20 for God bought you with a high price. So, you must honor God with your body.

Right off the bat, I don't know about you but growing up I never saw porn as a problem. All my friends were watching it, and, on any night, you could see sex on TV or in a movie theatre. Don't let me stay up late enough to catch some XXX HBO specials or BET UNCUT. Man, I was a happy young boy. So, what's the big deal? Isn't sex what men and women were made to do, why can't we watch it?

That was my mentality and it seemed harmless to watch at first, but after years of addiction I can attest that if not freed from this perverted desire, you will live a life of misery and emptiness. See, what your friends, coworkers, brothers, homeboy's, or family may not tell you is that porn is not solely the problem. The problem is the lustful desire within us that draws us to it. Therefore, this chapter is going to break down the major impact watching porn can have on one's life and the lustful desires that lead up to it, while providing information and practical steps to overcome it. Here is my story.

Nosiness is of the Devil, lol

Entering the new environment of high school, I would come to learn a lot about porn. I learned that there were people who sold it out of barbershops, car trunks, school lockers, and that you could access it at any time online for free. By my 12th grade year, I still had not had sex, but boy could I talk about it. I knew how to act like I knew what I was doing, and I had quite a way of causing girls to believe me, but honestly, I was terrified. However, during my 12th grade year I noticed that I would create a new account on various sites daily in order to get a free 1-hour viewing. I had gotten to the point that I needed to watch it. I had grown dependent on it so much that there was something that it gave me. There was more than a physical pleasure that I gained from it. There was now a sense of validation, affirmation, comfort, and security found in this crazy world of fantasy.

The Brain vs. Porn

I've now come to learn that what I was experiencing wasn't just an excitement to watch sex. Due to constant exposure to porn, my brain had created new connections within itself wherein porn was no longer about pleasure but a need and a part of my actual life. There is a connection between the amount a person views porn and the information that the brain receives so let's go a little deeper into this science.

What I'm about to share with you is pretty dope and will explain how one can get addicted to anything that brings them an intensive amount of pleasure. Writer of the Fight the New Drug website start the discussion on the way the brain reacts to porn by saying, "Rats, humans, and all mammals have something in their brain called a "reward center. Part of the reward center's job is to promote healthy living by rewarding you when you do something that either keeps you alive (e.g., eating), creates a new life (e.g., sex), or enriches your life (e.g., building satisfying relationships). The way it rewards you is by pumping a cocktail of "pleasure chemicals" through your brain"

(fightthenewdrug.org).

The writer continues by saying, "Those chemicals do more than make you feel great. While you're enjoying that good feeling, your brain is also building new nerve pathways to connect the pleasure you're feeling to the activity you're doing. It's the brain's way of making sure that whatever you're doing, you'll come back to it again." Now tell me this is not crazy. Our brains are so advanced that not only can they send chemicals to reward our bodies when we are doing something healthy or worthwhile, they also retain information of the action that causes the pleasure in order to draw us back to it in the future. The brain is so vast in its capabilities that humans aren't even able to use it in its full capacity. However, though the brain is so amazing, and it can track pleasure to a specified healthy action, it also can trace counterfeit actions such as smoking, drinking, viewing porn, and use it to send pleasure to the brain as well.

DeltaFosB, a protein which is pumped out by the reward center and set off by dopamine is responsible for building new nerve pathways to mentally connect what someone is doing to the pleasure he or she feels. "But DeltaFosB has another Job, and this is why its nickname is "the molecular switch for addiction." If enough DeltaFosB builds up, it flips a genetic switch, causing lasting changes in the brain that leave the user more vulnerable to addiction". (Fightthenewdrug.org).

This DeltaFosB protein is also so potent that it forms detailed associations with the experience called "cues". Fight The New Drug writer elaborates on these cues by saying, "For a porn consumer, it may be the memory of a porn scene or a place or time of day he or she can be alone with the internet. For an addict, the whole world starts to seem like a collection of cues and triggers leading them back to their addiction. Gradually, the porn pathways become sensitized, meaning they are easily triggered by the cues that are all around."

Now I must tell you about CREB, which stands for: cyclic adenosine monophosphate response element binding protein. When the brain is overloaded with dopamine, the brain will release CREB to defend itself. About CREB one writes, "CREB is like the brakes on a runaway reward center; it slows the pleasure response. With CREB onboard, porn that once excited a person stops having the same effect". It continues in saying, "Even other things that used to make them happy, like going out with friends or playing a favorite game, stop providing enjoyment because of the dulling effects of CREB. They experience strong cravings and often find themselves giving more of their time and attention to porn, sometimes to the detriment of relationships, school, or work."

These facts are very real and were heavily apparent in my life to the point that I had grown so dependent on porn that It took the place of what I lacked in my real life. Porn had somehow made me a man. It made up for what other people didn't say and gave me a sense of being. See I was no longer watching it for entertainment; but I found myself getting lost in the world of fantasy so deep that I could become the men on the screen. Once I was able to become them, then I felt like I was somebody. I was able to be confident, strong, and sexy. I was able to prove everybody wrong about me, and honestly, I was able to fill the void of love that was missing. I don't know what may have driven you to watch porn, may be tempting you to watch it now, or if you've never watched it all, but for me, there was a deep desire for love, belonging, and security and porn provided it all.

As you can see, there were many insecurities in me as a child and into my young adult years that had not been dealt with. This left me open and vulnerable, looking for love and validation in anything that would give me attention. Have you ever struggled with feeling loved or secure? Have you ever desired to escape from your current reality and enter a new life of endless possibilities? Well I did, and that's what drove me to watch porn more and more, not knowing that I was chasing fulfillment that could never be satisfied.

In today's society sex is everywhere and highly publicized as casual and without restriction, but light-porn through the forms of magazines, social media posts, and other media outlets are making it hard to avoid exposure to this type of epidemic. Dave Chaffey, writer of the article Global Social Media Research Summary 2019, presents fascinating facts about the internet, social media, and mobile phone usage. In this article he writes, "The number of internet users worldwide in 2019 is 4.388 billion, up 9.1% year-on-year", and continues by saying, "The number of social media user worldwide in 2019 is 3.484 billion, up 9% year-on-year". I present these facts because if we are not careful, our weaknesses will be exploited by Satan and the tentacles of lust and perversion will wrap around our souls and hinder the clarity of our identity and our intimacy with God.

Please don't take this lightly because lust has an assignment to kill us and destroy our ability to get to heaven. Moreover, I wish I could say that Satan played fair and waited until we got older to attack us with lust and perversion, but he doesn't, and often starts with our parents, grandparents, and great grands. Especially, if our forefathers didn't have the knowledge to understand spiritual matters and were prisoners to lust and perversion, it is possible that their demons were transferred to us and we are left to fight them in our lives. This is noted and proven in the first family of the bible. Look at how Adam and Eve started. Adam had a personal relationship with God where he would meet with God in the cool of the day and tend to his garden that was fruitful and filled with everything that he would ever need to sustain his life.

All was well, but God decided to give Adam a helper and created Eve out of his rib. Once they were together and after Adam had received instructions from God beforehand, they end up going against what God had said, introducing sin into the earth. Before this point, sin had not entered the earth and humanity was in perfect harmony with God, but upon their bad decision, disobedience brought about sin and disconnected man from God. This caused Adam to be pronounced to work in arduous terrain and Eve to experience terrible pains in her body for the rest of their lives. However, because of their disobedience, the sin of murder of covetousness was introduced to humanity through their sons Cain and Abel. Therefore, if you are a parent or you know that your parent may have struggled with lust or perversion and you see it active in your life, seek God for deliverance as it states in Psalms 34: 19(NLT) which says, "The righteous person faces many troubles, but the LORD comes to the rescue each time."

As I got older and through my initial college years, I was busy with classes, football games, band competitions, and other extracurricular activities that I no longer needed to watch porn and really didn't have the time. By this time, I'd had sex with a few girls and my self-confidence was higher, so I was feeling good for myself, but when I joined the Navy things changed. Having to leave Georgia in order to be stationed in Norfolk, VA was a major culture shock and left me alone, but I found my way around. I met a lot of new people and I was excited about my new job, but that void was back again and the desire to watch porn was way stronger than it was before.

This time I found myself having porn on every electrical device including my phone, tablet, and laptop. Not only did I have it on all my devices, the desire was so strong that I would watch it while I was driving, in my sleeping quarters aboard my ship, in public places, and restrooms. It was out of my control and I could not stop it. Even when I would promise myself that I wouldn't watch it for a certain amount of days, after a day or two, I would be back at it. So, what was once something that boys do turned into a full-blown addiction that was causing me more harm than good and I had no way to escape from the thing that used to be my escape. It was no longer fun, it was prison!

Walking in the Flesh is Dangerous!

Romans 8: 5-7(NLT)

"Those who are dominated by the sinful nature think about sinful things, but those who are controlled by the Holy Spirit think about things that please the Spirit. So letting your sinful nature control your mind leads to death. But letting the Spirit control your mind leads to life and peace. For the sinful nature is always hostile to God. It never did obey God's laws, and it never will."

Here in this passage we see that the first scripture points out a very key principle and gives hope to one who is struggling with the desires of their flesh by letting us know that we aren't just led by the flesh, we make a decision to follow it. This may be disheartening to some but relieving for others because by understanding that you don't have to live in bondage to the sins of your flesh and that you have the power to choose to be free, is empowering. It may seem that one's desire and addiction to porn is far beyond stopping but know that with God's help, you can defeat it. The second verse then exposes a horrific but relieving truth about one's choice of following the flesh or the spirit by giving us the result. If we choose to walk in a carnal or fleshly mind we will die, but if we choose to walk in the spirit we shall live. This death is not physical, this death denotes one of a spiritual, emotional, and psychological manner. See sin has a way of separating us from God because it makes us unclean.

Lust has an Assignment

James 1: 15(NLT) says, "These desires give birth to sinful actions. And when sin can grow, it gives birth to death." So, let's check out the progression of this verse. It starts out by saying, "When lust is conceived." See all the devil wants us as men to do is be trapped in a cycle of lust. He wants us to notice every woman, every curve, and every sundress, because if he can keep us distracted by our lustful desires, which are common to our flesh, we will separate ourselves from God.

Since our natural animalistic nature thrives off and responds more quickly to the pleasures of the flesh, we are more likely and drawn to fleshly things than spiritual things. It Is in our DNA to hunt, to prowl, to conquer and to rule, therefore, if we are not careful and do not allow the Holy Spirit to help us control our impulses, we will hopelessly fall to the flesh and hinder our ability to please God. So, do you see the trap? Just as Adam and Even in the beginning, who after their disobedience, were banished from the Garden of Eden and sentenced to hard labor and labor pains for the rest of their lives. It wasn't the fruit itself that was the sin, it wasn't even speaking to the serpent that was the sin; the sin was their disobedience to God's instruction which caused them to be separated from their promise.

This separation from God is what the world does not promote and is the root of why the porn industry has become so big. The Enough is Enough website states that every minute there are 63, 992 new visitors to the Pornhub website. It goes on to state, "Visits to Pornhub totaled 33.5 billion over the course of 2018, an increase of 5 billion visits over 2017. That equates to a daily average of 92 million visitors and at the time of this writing"

(https://enough.org/stats_porn_industry)

Writers on the Fight the New Drug website wrote an article titled 20 MInd-Blowing Stats About The Porn Industry And Its Underage Consumers also continues in the effort of addressing the stats of the Porn Industry by saying, "Porn is a global, estimated $97 Billion Industry, with about $12 billion of that coming from the U.S." (https://fightthenewdrug.org/10-pron-stats-that-will-blow-your-mind/). Then they go on to state, "A 2015 meta-analysis of 22 studies from seven countries found that internationally the consumption of pornography was significantly associated with increases in verbal and physical aggression, among males and females alike."

These are truly astounding numbers to digest and are eye opening to how progressive the pornographic epidemic has become. Researching its damage, I've learned that someone who continuously views porn is more likely to change their viewing preference from their initial preference. Fight the new Drug website says it this way, "Frequent porn consumption tends to escalate. Because of porn's addictive nature, porn consumers usually need an ever-increasing dosage over time in order to feel the same level of enjoyment, and they often have to seek out more extreme and hard-core forms of porn". Then it goes on to say, "Porn consumers can reach a point where they enjoy porn less and less but want it more and more". This means that the more one watches porn, the less pleasure they get from it, but the more they must have it. Their brain has been so hardwired to the feeling that porn provides that it can no longer survive without it even though they find no pleasure in it.

See the porn industry wants you to enjoy the free viewing, provocative marketing, and exotic promotions but they're not telling viewers that if they are not careful, they will lose their relationships with God due to their addiction. They are not telling their viewers that if they are not careful, they will become addicted to a false sense of reality that will cause them to lose their families, friends, relationships, and resources. Porn has become so familiar and common that it has been embraced and accepted to be a part of a young boy's life and if he has not viewed it or refuses to, he is an outcast. It is noted that, "64% of young people, ages 13-24, actively seek out pornography weekly or more of teen". "Teenage girls and young women are significantly more likely to actively seek out porn than women 25 years old and above", and "Porn sites receive more regular traffic than Netflix, Amazon, & Twitter combined each month" (Fightthenewdrug.org).

How many young boys, girls, men, and women do you believe can withstand this type of pressure? How many young boys do you think can withstand the ridicule of being inexperienced sexually or one who has never viewed porn or even desires to. Unfortunately, in today's society and even back in my day, a boy who held up a standard for righteousness or even a man who stood his ground against these things was considered to be weird, strange, or even in some cases seen as a homosexual. I don't know many young boys who can withstand this type of pressure and continue to pursue their beliefs, but I know many young men who fell to the temptation and now feel trapped and are unable to maintain healthy relationships with the opposite sex.

Porn hinders Real Relationships

Whether you are single, in a relationship, engaged, or married, porn can severely hinder the success of your relationship, and this is how. If we are not careful, we will subconsciously expect our partner to perform the same tricks, moves, and stunts that the girls were doing on the screen. We will also subconsciously find ourselves talking like the guys on the screen and treating our partners as they treated theirs. This is a dangerous place to be because in this place, you begin to treat your partner as a tool instead of a person or a wife.

Especially if you are married, you will carry your fantasy life into your marriage bed and destroy your ability to maintain a successful and thriving sex life.

How do I know, because it happened to me! When I got married, I already had all my moves ready! I knew what our first time was going to be like, and I was sure we were going to tear our room up! I felt like I had been preparing for that moment all my life, but when the time came my fantasy was shattered and I realized that my wife wasn't a girl on a screen that I could just have sex with. She was the woman that I loved, and vowed to cherish and to hold, and there was no way that I could treat her disrespectfully and have no regard for her body.

Not only does porn affect how you see your partner, but it also affects how you see yourself. By comparing yourself to the men on the screen, it is easy to judge your ability to perform based off of theirs. If you're not able to last as long as the men on the screen, get in certain positions, or take control like they do, It can drastically affect your self-confidence and your ability to perform without your partner having any complaint. This is important to understand because often when men grow up watching porn and enter a sexual relationship with someone, they begin to reenact what they saw on TV. Not only are they merely performing but they are unhappy while they are doing it because deep down on the inside, they aren't confident in themselves, they are confident in the ability of the man on the screen that they are mimicking. Not only do we fall into that trap, but we are also discouraged when we assume that our partner or wife desires us to perform porn star tricks and come to find out that they aren't interested in it at all.

Now if you and your wife share the type of sexual relationship that welcomes exotic or risky sex that is great and well with God, but if you try to force your wife to do something that she is not willing or ready for, you risk the danger of hurting or abusing her. I felt compelled to share my experiences and the truth of God's word with you because I truly believe that the acceptance of porn in our culture today has truly hindered the sanctity of marriage and is destroying what God called to be great. I will not stand back and allow lust, perversion, and sexual immorality to continue to destroy our image as men and I know that he can heal us from this gripping desire. Therefore, if you are one who struggles with this or believe that this could be a problem for you in the future don't be ashamed; I completely understand, and God does too. Continue to go to him and seek him with all of your heart and he will deliver you and cleanse of this stronghold.

While God is working on your heart, here are a few things you can do to protect yourself from becoming addicted or relapsing into an addiction:

1. <u>Be Honest:</u> A lot of men struggle with being honest about our weaknesses, struggles, or battles, but this is not one to play with. Until now, you may not have even seen watching porn as a bad thing, but if you have been convinced of the fact, take time to be honest with yourself and seek God for direction and deliverance.

2. <u>Trace Your triggers:</u> Find out what thoughts, places, or images cause you to think about perverted sex or porn and do your best to protect yourself from them.

a. For Example: If you know that watching certain music videos, scrolling on your Facebook timeline, looking at Instagram photos, or listening to certain types of music gets you into an unhealthy sexual mode; get away from them completely or for a time until you're able to entertain them without you drifting into unhealthy sexual thoughts.

b. If you start thinking about an ex who watched porn with you or encouraged it during intimate times, immediately stop what you're doing, and start to think about something that is more positive and healthier. When I find myself in thoughts like this I often stop and pray and quote the following scripture from Colossians which says, "Set your minds on things above, not on earthly things" (NLT).

3. <u>Get Help:</u> There are many Clinics, Hospitals, and Rehabilitations centers all throughout the world that focus on all types of addictions and healthy rehabilitation. Even if you don't want to take it that far, talk to a counselor, therapist, psychologist, Pastor, Family member, or somebody that you trust that can help you bare this burden and seek God on your behalf for your healing and deliverance. This is one of the most important steps to take because you never know who else is struggling with this and if you all join, you can be free together.

a. ABOVE ALL… Seek God, pray, worship, and walk in obedience to his word and he will deliver you. I don't even know exactly when I got delivered or stopped watching porn. All I know is back in 2011, when I gave my life to Christ for real and started walking in his ways, he started to take my old passions away and gave me new passions, new insight, and understand of who I am and who I am called to be.

4. <u>Block the Sites and Delete all Pre-Downloaded pornographic Material to include Videos & Pictures:</u> Now I had to do this myself! It was one of the hardest things I've had to do, but it was worth it because I deleted all the ties I had to porn. This is important because you have to protect yourself from yourself, and now having an understanding of how the brain reprograms itself to desire porn after continued exposure to it, it's going to eventually draw you back to it, and you have to protect yourself from falling for it again.

5. <u>Hang around People who don't watch Porn and stop Talking and Hanging out with those that Do:</u> I cannot express the value of this point! I'll just say this, the bible says, "As Iron sharpens Iron, so a friend sharpens a friend" (Proverbs 27: 17, NLT). This means that when you hang around strong people, you will get stronger, but when you hang around weaker people, you will get weaker or duller. Therefore, to protect yourself from temptation and sin until God appoints you to go back to them and tell them about your deliverance; take some time away to spend with God and allow a new group of people to fortify you and build you up.

I really pray that this information has blessed you with greater understanding, wisdom, and insight about this epidemic and is something that you can use to educate other people. It's unfortunate that our society is promoting something that is so deadly to our souls, but it is our job to teach the truths behind this growing epidemic and save others from this life debilitating disease. I love you man and I am excited about your future, but I am more impressed with your dedication to yourself today, so I applaud you and pray that God is with you everywhere that you go.

Right now, in the name of Jesus, I pray that the same way Jesus Christ supernaturally delivered me from this dreadful addiction, that he performs that same miracle in you right now. In the name of Jesus Christ, I pray that your brain is reprogrammed back to its original state and on the trauma that it faced from repeated exposure is erased. I pray healing to your soul and restoration in your mind and I declare that you shall prosper and be in good health, just as your soul prospers. In the Name of Jesus Christ, I pray, Amen!

CHAPTER 6
THE 5 P'S (PRIOR PREPARATION PREVENTS POOR PERFORMANCE)

"If you fail to prepare, you prepare to fail"

-Benjamin Franklin

Have you ever pursued a dream, goal, or passion without first seeking out the proper information, training, or qualifications necessary to be successful in it? Let me ask you one more question and please be honest: Have you ever gotten into a relationship with someone without first finding out who they were and if they were possibly an undercover psycho? You don't have to lie Craig; you don't have to lie! But what I'm trying to find out is, how many things have you started or pursued without properly preparing for it? How did that venture, goal, or relationship end up? Did it meet your expectations and if it didn't, how did the disappointment affect your confidence?

I ask these questions because I've learned that properly preparing for a new phase of life, venture, relationship, or idea will not only affect the longevity of what you're pursuing, but it will also immensely affect your self-confidence if that new thing fails. In this chapter, I am going to share with you a few principles about the importance of preparation, its positive results if applied properly and the negative results if not applied at all. Are you ready? Let's begin!

Excitement is Deceptive!

If you're anything like me, you love the idea of pursuing new things. Whether it is a new building project, college course, relationship, business deal, book, or investment opportunity. You get excited when you are presented with new things. I know this all too well because I have a tendency of getting excited about new things and starting new projects then a few days later I've stopped working out and I'm back to eating Chic-fil-a. After I get done eating that number 2 deluxe with no tomatoes and lettuce and add bacon, a small bit of guilt emerges from within because I am reminded that I have started something, and failed to complete it again. What I want to submit to you is that properly preparing for new things in your life will not only position you to attain greater levels of success, but it will also boost your level of confidence. No one desires to fail, everyone desires to succeed and complete the tasks that they set out to reach but many people seldomly take the time to create a plan to guide their success.

I'm going to be like my Daddy

In today's society, we as men are raised from childhood to believe that it is our duty to grow up and to be the provider, protector, and breadwinner for our homes. From as early as 10 years old, some of us had the privilege of watching our father, or a father figure work hard, provide for his family, make sure that there was food on the table, and do all he could to be there for us but some of us didn't. Others were either left with a father in the home that was not the best example or forced to admire a male figure that was in the lives of others because our father wasn't in our home.

Well for me, I can identify with the latter and grew up believing that once I was married with kids, I would be their provider and their protector but boy was I in for a treat. Now at this moment I need you to buckle up your seat belt because in this chapter I'm going to share with you how I almost ruined my first marriage by telling my wife that God told me to get out of the military to pursue my vision as an entrepreneur. I don't know if you've ever been in a situation like this or maybe have made decisions off of impulse or pure zeal without proper consideration, but if so, this chapter is for you. So here it goes.

The date is some time in 2016 when I told my ex-wife that God said that I was getting out of the military to pursue my calling as an entrepreneur. Now mind you, at this time I had no business, product, or service to provide and on top of that I had no business training or qualifications at all, but let me tell you something, I knew it was God. So, I confidently told my wife and everybody that would listen. I was flaunting and boasting to everybody for months about all my future plans and all my planned accomplishments. Man, you couldn't tell me nothing. A couple more months go by and 2017 comes and I'm still excited and ready to pursue my dreams.

It was almost time for me to get out and I found myself panicking and constantly nervous and wondering what life was going to be like once I got out. Now, a few months before I was extremely confident but all of a sudden that excitement turned to pure panic that I couldn't share with others because by now, I had talked so much that if I went back to say that God didn't say it, I would look like a fool.

So, one night a few members from my church and I went to go fellowship with another church during their Leadership conference. This conference was amazing, and the message was phenomenal, but in the middle of the service God told me that it wasn't the time and I had sped up the time out of zeal and excitement. You must love God for what he does because he won't allow you to jack up your life to bad without him intervening. So that night I went and told my wife and apologized to her for putting her through the stress and aggravation of having to listen and watch me stress about something that was out of season.

One of the ways I could've known that I was not properly prepared was by knowing that I didn't have a thorough plan that laid out the strategies I was going to take to ensure my success. About this Napoleon HIll, author of the book Think and Grow Rich writes, "Your achievement can be no greater than your plans are sound" (1960, p. 83). Then later he goes on to write, "The successful leader must plan his work, and work his plan" (p. 85). Another way I could've known that I wasn't prepared for my success is by knowing that I didn't have a team to work the vision with me. About this Hill relays a valid point by saying, "No individual has sufficient experience, education, native ability, and knowledge to insure the accumulation of a great future, without the cooperation of other people. Every plan you adopt, in your endeavor to accumulate wealth, should be the joint creation of yourself and every other member of your "Master Mind" group" (p. 82). I will go into further detail about planning and creating a team for the job later in this chapter, but let's continue.

Build a Foundation

Now I must tell you that God did say what I said he said; however It wasn't at the time that I had made it out to be. He spoke through various prophets, pastors, and people of God proclaiming the entrepreneurial lifestyle that I would come to live, but with pride instead of wisdom I attempted to birth something out of season. I share this with you to introduce my first principle: Build a foundation! What do I mean by build a foundation? A foundation is defined as the lowest load-bearing part of a building, typically below ground level. This definition is great for you to understand and to apply because the foundation is the most important part of your entire life.

Think about a house. A house could have a beautiful kitchen, roof, bathroom, and garage, but, if the foundation is messed up the house is in trouble and the same principle applies to you. If you do not build a firm foundation of understanding, faith, work ethic, consistency, and determination which is all found from within, you will not be successful. Therefore, your foundation is essential to the enhancement of your personal, spiritual, emotional, and psychological development. Luke 14: 28(NLT) says it this way, "But don't begin until you count the cost. For who would begin construction of a building without first calculating the cost to see if there is enough money to finish it?" In this verse, building the building is not the issue. Even desiring to build the building is not the issue. The issue is one's inability to sit down and properly prepare by planning out and researching the things necessary to build the building.

Let me go ahead and expose myself and some of my silly ways. While away in Lakehurst, New Jersey, for some extended military training I had a great idea of starting my own t-shirt design company. So, I went to Wal-Mart and picked up all the graphic design and paint supplies that I needed. I also picked up the top of the line t-shirts that they carried and excitedly hurried back to my hotel. When I got there, I immediately laid out all my t-shirts and went to work. Man, this was amazing; I was finally doing something, however, little did I know this new venture would soon fail. After a few minutes of spraying, painting, designing, and sweating, I realized that t-shirt design was not my thing. Now you would think that a person who had just got an idea the morning of, who didn't have any design experience, and was not the best in arts in crafts would know that their possibility of success would be minimal, but I didn't care. All I wanted to do was create, inspire, and make my mark on the world but I soon realized that t-shirt design was not my calling so remember to first: Build your foundation!

Building your foundation is simply first understanding what you want to do, learning what it takes to do accomplish it, connecting with people who have done it already or have experience in your specific field/interest, and believing that you can do it. In the example I gave you before I failed to perform any of these steps and went about it off my own knowledge which made me incapable of being as successful as I could've been. There are many people who are wildly successful at making graphic t-shirts and things like that, but there is a difference between investing in an idea and a dream.

An idea will lead you down a rabbit whole of much disappointment, but what I want to teach you in this book is to seek God for his vision and plan for your life because when you get it, you won't have to fund it alone. That morning I was so excited that I didn't think, I just went off impulse. Which in hindsight caused me to waist money, time, and energy in an area that I was never called to do. Therefore, take the time to build your foundation because it will not only elevate your self-confidence, but it will guarantee a greater probability of success in any area of interest you have.

1. Write a Vision/ Create a Plan

After you have done your research and built your foundation it's time to Write a Vision and Create a Plan! Habakkuk 2:2 of the King James Version says, "And the Lord answered me, and said, Write the vision, and make it plain upon tables, that he may run that readeth it." This scripture lets us know that it is important to write down our ideas, thoughts, and desires because once they are written they are established. However, writing them down is only the first step. The latter part of this scripture states, "that he may run that readeth it;" this lets us know that we must write our visions, dreams, and ideas down in an instructional and strategic planning format that will work to keep us focused and goal driven within the desired amount of time that we have allotted for ourselves. On this topic I once heard a preacher say that there is a difference between a dream and a goal. A goal has a definite execution date, and a dream does not, it is left up to possibility. Therefore, once you write your vision, be bold and write down a completion date, this will not only inspire you, but force you to be disciplined and make you sacrifice in order to make the date that you set for yourself.

For example, I started this book March of 2018 and I had a desired completion date of April 22, 2018. I typed it up and printed it out and placed it on my vision board at home. Today is April 1, 2018 and I am almost complete with the second chapter of this book. I share this with you because once I wrote down my vision and came up with a finishing date, my mentality changed from it being a great idea to "I have to get this done." I've begun to think this way not only because I want to finish this book but because I knew that there were other men out there that would benefit from it. When you identify who is attached to your vision, goal, or dream, that will be the push you need to proceed even when times get hard. So, keep dreaming and keep working.

To continue on the topic of planning, Napoleon Hill writes, "If the first plan which you adopt doesn't work successfully, replace it with a new plan; if this new plan fails to work, replace it in turn with still another, and so on, until you find a plan which does work" (p. 83). Then he goes on to say, "Right here is the point at which the majority of men meet with failure, because of their lack of persistence in creating new plans to take the place of those which fail" (p. 83). I have experienced this myself. When you give your heart and soul to something and it fails, you don't often have the strength or courage to sit down and write up a new plan. This also keeps us from working on our first plan which we're never able to complete because we are afraid that it will fail. The thought of having to replace the first plan with a second one keeps us in bondage so much so that we end up not accomplishing anything because we are bound by the fear of failure.

Prior planning is so important and is relevant to everyone. Whether one is pursuing a relationship, degree, new job opportunity, or business, but it is especially true in business. About this Jennifer Lee, author of the book The Right-Brain Business Plan; A Creative, Visual Map for Success writes, "Think about it. If your business plan is a road map to your success, then not having a plan is like driving without directions to an unknown destination- yikes" (2011, p. 2). Then she goes on to write, "When planning seems unappealing, it doesn't get done, and that can derail your business. In fact, the Small Business Administration estimates that 50 percent of small businesses in America fail within their first five years. Lack of planning is often to blame" (p. 3). Therefore, if you are seeking to start a business or anything that will require you to expend your money, time, or service, please take time to plan and gain the greatest understanding you can in order to position yourself for a greater return on your personal investment.

One of the greatest things I love about the process of starting a business is the need for creating a business plan. Business plans can be long, drawn out, and hard work, but they can also be fun, creative, and provide a right now view of your future success. Though the process of planning is important for entrepreneurs, you can also take the same approach of planning into relationships. Did you know that you can have a vision for what your desired relationship is going to look like 5 to 10 years down the line? Did you know that you can create a vision board of your desired marriage? Well, you can and let me tell you a few things that you can put in it.

One of the first things you need in your relationship vision or plan is the description of your Love Language(s) and how you desire to be loved. The 5

Love Languages book, written by Gary Chapman, addresses 5 general ways that people desire to be loved and are important for each partner to know. These love languages include: Quality Time, Gift Giving, Physical Touch, Words of Affirmation, & Acts of Service. Understanding these will extremely benefit your relationship, but another facet of your plan should have your non-negotiables. Non-negotiables are the things that you are not willing to permit in a relationship. For example, If you don't like women who smoke, if you one where attempting to date you, you wouldn't be willing to do it because dating a woman who smokes is a no-go. I would love to expound on these right now, but I'll be writing forever; So, let's keep moving in the steps of Prior Preparation Prevents Poor Performance.

2. Build your Team

Habakkuk 2: 2 of the King James Version Bible says, "And the Lord answered me, and said, Write the vision, and make it plain upon tables, that he may run that readeth it". Check out the order of the process that is presented in this scripture. First, we write the vision, then we make sure it is concise and understandable in a strategic manner, then we present it to others to make it happen. Really look at the scripture and meditate on it. I've been reading it for years and have never had this clear of an understanding of it. The process of our development is in this scripture and shows us that we are not responsible for all three portions of the process of development. Sometimes God will give you the responsibility of creating a vision, ensuring that it is concise and written in a strategic manner, but it is someone else's job to carry it out.

This is one of the hardest things to do as a man and especially as a leader, because as leaders we are often control freaks and have a hard time trusting people. Consequently, we are left to write the vision and work it and we are never able to rest because it wasn't our job to work the vision, it was only our job to seek God and to write it, then hire or permit others to work it. So how should we go by creating a team for the task. Here are a few qualities that your team members should have:

● Believe in what you believe in:

○ Psalms 133: 1(NLT)- How wonderful and pleasant it is when brothers live together in harmony!

● Hard workers independently:

○ Proverbs 12: 24(NLT)- Work hard and become a Leader; be lazy and become a slave.

○ Proverbs 13: 4(NLT)- Lazy people want much but get little, but those who work hard will prosper.

● Knowledgeable/Skilled

○ Matthew 4: 19(NLT)- Jesus called out to them," Come, follow me, and I will show you how to fish for people."

● Willing to work in a Team

○ Amos 3:3(NLT)- Can two people walk together, without agreeing on the direction?

● Love God and others

○ Mark 12:30(NLT)- And you must love the Lord your God with all your heart, all your soul, all your mind, and all your strength.

○ 1 John 4: 18-19(NLT)- Such love has no fear, because perfect love expels all fear. If we are afraid, it is for fear of punishment, and this shows that we have not fully experienced his perfect. We love each other because he loved us first.

○ 1 Peter 4: 8(NLT)- Most important of all, continue to show deep love for each other, for love covers a multitude of sins.

Though these are only a few, they provide a great base to start looking for in your perspective team members and can help guide your selection process. Feel free to aid and customize your own team member qualification list because remember, whoever you allow into your circle can either positively or negatively affect your circumstances. Therefore, take some time to really think about what you desire in a team member and once you figure it out, let the process of selection begin.

3.Seek God then Go

Once you've built your foundation, written a vision, created a plan, and formed your team it's time to seek God then GO. You've worked hard, put in the time, and showed yourself and God that you are serious, so when He tells you to Go don't be afraid. It reminds me of the time in the bible when God told Abram in Genesis chapter 12 to leave his family, kindred, and his father's house and go to the place where he would show him. Now I don't know about you, but I don't know how I would respond to God if He told me to leave everything and everybody I love to go to a place that is unknown. But as I look over this request and understand that God wouldn't set him up for failure, I begin to see how God was setting Abram up for a major blessing. See, sometimes God hides blessings in unfamiliar places. Sometimes God will provoke you to trust him when you can't trace Him. Sometimes God will set you up to walk by faith without having any understanding of what's to come, but we know that all things will work together.

Honestly, this topic is simple to write to you, but it has been one of the hardest things to apply because I have a tendency of desiring to do everything. This has proven to be one of the main reasons why I've changed my major 5 times. It's not that I am unable to learn, it's because I failed to do the proper research on the majors that I chose so when I received my work and it was too hard or undesirable, I would give up and change to another one. Not only did I find myself making decisions without preparing in my educational pursuits, I also entered into business ventures and other opportunities without proper preparation.

So, what about you? Since you've been reading this chapter, have you been able to identify a few times that you have started something without properly preparing or are you currently pursuing something that you are somewhat unsure about? If so, it's okay, stop what you're doing, assess your environment, get the information you need to make yourself more stable in that area, or back out of it until you get the tools and resources you need to be successful and prevent damaging yourself, others, or an organization.

After you've done the work be prepared for God to give you the green light on that marriage, business, career, real estate purchase, degree, diploma, certification, ministry, church, or investment. Be prepared to move and trust that God will carry you all the way. I am currently smack dab during that right now. It is currently 12:36 a.m. on April 2, 2018, and no less than 30 minutes ago was I on the phone with my wife who told me that she had moved her stuff out of our home. I will go more into that a little bit later in the book but what I want you to know is that earlier this week God gave me the green light. He prepared me for this very moment and for that I am grateful. So now I am earnestly expecting what he has set for me in the future. So, go man of God and don't be afraid. You may not know it all or have all the answers. You may not have the degree or the proper qualifications.

You may not have the six-figure income or the s550 Mercedes Benz, but if God says go, GOOOOOO. Trust him and know that he prepared you and has predestined your life before the earth was created and the steps of a good man are ordered by the Lord.

ROBERT B. VANN

CHAPTER 7
LOW SELF-ESTEEM: A SILENT KILLER

Philippians 1: 6(NIV)

Being confident of this, that he who began a good work in you will carry it on to completion until the day of Christ Jesus.

There is nothing worse than being a man and not feeling like one. Many may not be able to confidently express this, but there is nothing worse than knowing that you are physically a man while simultaneously feeling incapable of doing what a man does. Often, those who feel incapable really aren't, they're just victims of misguided expectations and are holding themselves prison to an image that is impossible to fulfill. Even when one excels in an area that makes them feel more manly such as being in a relationship with a beautiful woman, finally getting a six pack, or driving a really nice car, they are unable to attain lasting fulfillment because their lack of esteem always moves the marker further and further away. This chapter I'm going to discuss the debilitating effects of low self-esteem and how it can destroy the life of any good man from the inside out, then provide principles to overcome it and walk in true God confidence.

External Success doesn't get rid of Low Self-Esteem

It's an unfortunate truth that many who are walking around day-by-day are unaware that they're living purposeless lives. They are taking care of their families, going to work, serving in church, helping in their communities, running their businesses, and covering their children, but haven't yet learned or tapped into the riches of who they are. For far too long I believe that many men have based their existence off of what they do and not who they are and are unable to see the difference. About this Mark Driscoll, author of the book Who Do You Think You are? Finding your identity in Christ writes, "You aren't what's been done to you but what Jesus has done for you. You aren't what you do but what Jesus has done. What you do doesn't determine who are" (2013, p. 3). HIs words hit a point that I believe is important to understand because for so long, even myself, I based my existence purely off what I did, instead of who I was and didn't even know why. I also didn't know who to go to or where I could go to find an answer.

Mark Driscoll, however, continues in this discussion by saying, "This world's fundamental problem is that we don't understand who we truly are- children of God made in his image- and instead define ourselves by any number of things other than Jesus" (p. 2). Therefore, the first point I bring up is that the cure of low self-esteem can only be found in Jesus Christ and is simple to attain. However, as men, we pride ourselves on building new engines, developing great financial portfolios, buying new homes, marrying beautiful women, and other things that people can see, but none of those things can solve the problem of low self-esteem. Some men strive to be successful on the outside in order to prevent anyone from knowing how they feel on the inside. I know this to be true because I believed that if I achieved more on the outside that it would make me feel better about myself on the inside but that was false.

As time has progressed, I've learned that there is a difference between investing in yourself in order to love yourself compared to investing in yourself because you love yourself. For example, let's say you were insecure about your weight which caused you to feel inadequate and uncomfortable with your appearance which resulted in constant feelings of low self-esteem and low self-worth. So, you start working out expecting that once you get the body you want, you will feel better about yourself. However, once you get the body you want you find that your hidden underlying issue of perfection won't even allow you to enjoy the results of your labor. You will still find reasons not to accept yourself because you work to find imperfections in the changes that you've made. Consequently, a close relative to low self-esteem is perfectionism, and perfectionism is an impossible void they cannot be filled.

One of the scariest things about low self-esteem is that it can go untraceable for years without being detected. Someone in your family, on your job, or in your class can go years struggling with it without you ever knowing it because a person with low self-esteem is ashamed and will do everything they can to protect themselves from being vulnerable around others who can see their insecurity. This is why you must look within yourself and be honest enough to admit that you battle with low self-esteem, you must do this because it will ruin your life and lock you in a place of shame and bitterness where no one will be able to you don't or get you out. Low self-esteem is so restricting that it causes many to suffer from anxiety attacks, deep seated depression, weight loss/gain, comparison issues, and many other debilitating emotional effects that breed thoughts of negativity and put physical stress on the body and heart.

What is Low Self-Esteem?

A UC Davis Health article titled Self-Esteem defines and describes Low Self-esteem by saying, "Low self-esteem is defined as a debilitating condition that keeps individuals from realizing their full potential. A person with low self-esteem feels unworthy, incapable, and incompetent." It also goes on to say that many people who struggle with low self-esteem often deal with anxiousness and fear.

Reading this I see that I've dealt with low self-esteem most of my life and that growing up I often felt less than, unwanted, and an inconvenience. Have you ever felt this way? If, so, how have these feelings affected your adult life? For me, Low Self-esteem has immensely affected my adult life in a negative way. As a husband, leader, sailor, brother, preacher, author, and speaker, low self-esteem has caused me to miss out on countless opportunities, loose relationships, struggle with my sexuality, battle with pornography, and mostly devastating, live a life less than what God has ordained me to live. However, I speak to you right now declaring that you can live beyond this bondage. You can live beyond these negative emotions. You can live beyond the pain and struggle of feeling inadequate. You can live a life of knowing who you are, and you shall in the name of Jesus Christ!

Dig up the root!

As the definition of low self-esteem states, it is a debilitating condition that keeps individuals from realizing their full potential. This statement is 100% true but it leads me to ask the question, where does low self-esteem come from? We're not born hating ourselves or seeing ourselves as less than and I'm sure that our parents didn't intentionally sit us down and teach us how to feel unworthy, incapable, or incompetent. So, where does it come from? For me, low self-esteem was the result of living in a broken home. Living in a single parent home without the physical presence of my father truly affected me but it wasn't always that way.

Between the ages of around 3-5, I can remember living in an apartment building right outside of the Fort Sill army base with my mom and dad in Lawton, Oklahoma. It was nice there, but the weather was crazy. Time passed and my father got orders to Fort Benning in Columbus, GA so we packed up and moved. This seemed to be a great move, but something was different. Though we moved to a new place filled with great opportunity, I saw less and less of my father. He would get sent to Afghanistan for a year, then Korea, then

Kuwait, then back to Korea, then he stopped coming home totally and after a few years I was introduced to the term of separation. My parents were now separated and would later be divorced when I was 13 in the 9th grade. Not only were they divorced but my father would later marry a woman who had 5 kids.

Now this may not seem big to you but Imagine how I felt as his only biological child, who would later come to know that his father who had left his mother, married someone else who had five kids and was also in the military. I thought he abandoned me and left us to do his on thing. Though this wasn't the case, I was crushed, angry, and mad at the world and didn't know who to blame. I didn't know whether to blame, myself, or my mother, so naturally due to my immaturity I blamed my mother.

I may continue with this story later, but I had to present it to you now for you to understand my next point. When my father left, I felt rejected, abandoned, and placed the responsibility of their separation on me. Therefore, I felt unworthy, unloved, unprotected, and the cause of everyone's problem around me. Because of this, I took on the notion to make everyone's life around me better. I became a perfectionist. What are perfectionists? Merriam-Webster defines a Perfectionism as a disposition to regard anything short of perfection as unacceptable. This means that a perfectionist will not be satisfied until everything around them and even themselves is perfect. Whether it is their hair, body, make up, marriage, car, or social media image.

Perfectionism is so controlling that a person who suffers from it is very seldomly happy. Their constantly looking at their lives through the lenses of perfection and if they see that something isn't right they are tormented within until the problem is fixed, unfortunately, many of us are unable to experience the true peace of God because our perfectionist disposition and it is leading us instead of the spirit of God.

Website, Psychology Today, hosts a article titled Perfectionism which provides great insight on perfectionism and its effects on our daily lives; in this article the author writes, "Perfectionism is a trait that makes life an endless report card on accomplishments or looks. A fast and enduring track to unhappiness, it is often accompanied by depression and eating disorders. What makes perfectionism so toxic is that while those in its grip desire success, they are most focused on avoiding failure, so theirs is a negative orientation" (https://www.psychologytoday.com/us/basics/perfectionism). Then it goes on to say, "And love isn't a refuge; in fact, it feels way too conditional on performance. Perfection, of course, is an abstraction, an impossibility in reality, and often it leads to procrastination."

Now check this out, remember how I said before that perfectionism and low self-esteem are related, let me show you how. When one suffers from perfectionism, they set impossible standards that they can't reach, therefore, it is in that failure to reach those standards that many fall into low self-esteem. As stated before, low self-esteem is derived from a person feeling incapable, incompetent, and unworthy and one of the worst times in anyone's life is when they fail to accomplish something that they set out to do. It is the space between setting a goal and its completion that is the breeding ground for low self-esteem. It is the space between having parents and feeling accepted by them that is the breeding ground for low self-esteem. It is the space between having a wife, girlfriend, or even children and feeling unloved by them that is the breeding ground for low self-esteem.

Challenge: I challenge you to shorten the gaps that you have in your life by asking the right questions and doing the right things. If you see that there is a gap in your relationship with your spouse or kids, shorten the gap by communicating with them, get understanding, and create a strategy that brings fulfillment to you and the parties that are involved. If there is a gap between you and the completion of a vision, dream, degree, or business; take the time to assess where you are, where you desire to be, and write down a list of small tasks that you can do to bring that desire to pass. After you do that, start completing those tasks and watch how your confidence yourself grows and your disposition towards yourself and your abilities change from negative to positive!

In response to perfectionism, low self-esteem, and the gaps in my life, I made it may duty to make friends and to be nice because I couldn't take being left again. My low self-esteem was derived out of rejection and abandonment, therefore, I would do whatever I had to do to keep anyone else from leaving me again, even if I had to forsake my beliefs. Consequently, low self-esteem will make you adjust your priorities, values, and morals to fit in or to be accepted which is more often found in woman, but men struggle with this notion more than we would like to admit.

Even as a husband, I became a "Yes Man" not because I wanted too, but because I served out of fear instead of love. Yes, I said serve! I became what one would call "The Food Guy", you know the guy that a woman contacts only for the man to purchase them some food. My value was so low, that I lowered myself to an errand boy instead of a husband and my daily conversations with her were centered around what I could do for her instead of what I needed for me. Now this was not a position that she put me in, I put myself in this and reduced my value because I didn't understand who and whose I was. Reducing myself was not a form of humility or grace, low self-esteem is truly a form of pride in reverse.

See our pride as men and the pressures of life put us in the position to show no weakness in the midst of pain. It's gotten so bad that if a man reveals that he is hurt or upset that he is categorized as weak or even feminine. Therefore, knowing this, most men will put on a persona of strength and over exaggerate their masculinity in order to protect themselves from this type of attack and emotional assault. Have you ever felt this way? How many times have you swallowed your emotions in order to seem strong? How many times have you attempted to communicate your emotions but were mishandled due to the lack of understanding from the one(s) listening? Whether it's from a spouse, boss, friend, coworker, or whoever, this type of treatment as adult men coupled with the trauma that we've faced as young boys has positioned a lot of us to be victims of low self-esteem and has terrified us to admit it. Well you don't have to be afraid anymore because with the help of God, he will establish your identity and restore your confidence so that you will be able to live a life of happiness and true fulfillment. So, Let's begin.

True Happiness is in God!

In order to truly gain and walk in happiness and fulfillment, you must first stop striving to please people. Everybody will not like, agree, or support you but God always will. God always has your back and he will never leave you nor forsake you. This scripture will help you to understand that there is a limitation to what man can do for you. No matter how much your mother, father, wife, kids, boss, or subordinates try to love and support you, they are destined to fail and disappoint you and surprisingly God created us that way on purpose.

He did this so that we would not look to each other as gods and place people in his place. I made this mistake in my marriage. I placed her at such a high regard and desired her love and acceptance so much that I sought her attention more than I sought Gods. I sought her presence more than I sought God. I desired to have sex with her more than I desired to worship God and in turn I was constantly disappointed, rejected, and hurt wondering what I was doing wrong. I didn't understand that even though I was doing the right thing to ensure the safe and well-being of my wife that I was sinning and made her an idol and so my marriage struggled and eventually ended while my confidence got lower and lower.

Psalm 146:3-5 King James Version (NLT)

Don't put your confidence in powerful people; there is no help for you there. When they breathe their last, they return to the earth, and all their plans die with them. But joyful are those who have the God of Israel as their helper, whose hope is in the LORD their God.

Verse 3 of Psalms chapter 146 gives us great insight to the limitations of man. The bible tells us to look to the hills from which are help comes from and this verse backs it up back saying that there is no help in man or mankind. Yes, we can satisfy each other's physical needs and may be able to help spiritually and mentally as well but our true help can only come from God. Verse 4 explains to us that once a person dies, their breath and their thoughts end. Think about this, when a person passes away their breath and their thoughts end. So why would we allow what people think to control us, while they are alive. If you were afraid of someone and could only get freedom when they passed away, that would be a miserable life. But in God, he allows us to live in freedom and in true happiness when we simply put God as our helper and our hope. This simply means that we ought to value God's words more than the words of man.

Now what does this do? I'll tell you! When you compare God's words to the words of others and even your own, you will find that God has a higher regard for you than you think. His word says that you are the head and not the tail, above only and not beneath. God's word says that you are fearfully and wonderfully made in his image and nothing can pluck you out of his hands. Therefore, anyone or any thought that you may have that doesn't line up or agree with what God says about you is a lie and doesn't belong. I don't care if you have been telling yourself that you don't belong and are an outcast, guess what, Psalms 27: 10(NLT) says, "Even if my mother and my father abandon me, the LORD will hold me close." Therefore, don't settle for what you or what others think about you. Seek God and allow what he says about you to elevate your confidence and change your entire perspective about you.

True Love is in God

1 John 4:19 (NLT)

"We love each other because he loved us first."

Many people may not believe this, but men need love too! I don't care how much we accomplish, how macho we are, or how serious we put off being, men need love to, and we also want to feel safe. As much as I refused to admit it, I've been searching for love all my life. Even as an adult male who has been married for 6 years and serves in ministry, I've been searching for love for years. I thought when I got married, I would feel loved, but It wasn't enough. I thought that as I became a leader in the church and began preaching, I would feel loved, but I didn't. I thought that as I served and helped other people that I would feel loved, but that didn't work either. However, I've found that true sustainable love can only be found in God. God's love is different than man's love because God's love doesn't require anything back.

God's love doesn't require you to be perfect, smart, religious, or strong. God's love is unconditional and everlasting. Meaning, no matter what you do, God will still love you. No matter where you are, God will still love you. No matter who you are with, God will still love you. Even when you turn your back on him God will still love you, therefore, you should love yourself and God because if he can love you, you should love yourself too.

You are a Son of God

Psalm 27:10-14 New International Version (NIV)

Even if my father and mother abandon me, the Lord will hold me close. Teach me how to live, O Lord. Lead me along the right path, for my enemies are waiting for me. Do not let me fall into their hands. For they accuse me of things I've never done; with every breath they threaten me with violence. Yet I am confident I will see the Lord's goodness while I am here in the land of the living. Wait patiently for the Lord. Be brave and courageous. Yes, wait patiently for the Lord.

I leave this point until last because no matter what you do or how you feel about yourself, you are a Son of God. Though you may have been rejected by your parents, friends, family, or loved ones, God loves you and will never leave you nor forsake you. I want you to know that no matter who has left, dropped, abandoned, or rejected you; you matter, and you belong. I didn't realize how important these words would matter to me and lift my spirits but knowing that I matter has changed my life. Understanding that the reason for my father leaving and results of my parents' marriage wasn't my fault freed me from the life of shame, hurt, and rejection I once carried.

I don't know if you may have struggled with this type of rejection, abandonment, or frustration but know today that you can be healed from it. Whether you are single, married, or even divorced, you can be healed, and your confidence can be restored. Know that if you bring your hurt to God, He will heal you because you are His son. He understands how you feel and desires to be your Lord today.

I know this all too well because I write to you today, March 08, 2019, as a divorced man. I was married for 7 years to an amazing woman, but It didn't work out. The shame, guilt, lowliness, and emotional battles that come with this type of decision and experience can be paralyzing and prevent even the strongest person from bouncing back. But I tell you right now, that I am stronger and more confident now than I've ever been. You may not understand what I'm about to say but, my divorce saved my life. It showed me how low I was. It showed me how fragile I was. It showed me how afraid I was, and how much I needed God to do as stated in Psalm 27: 10-14, I need him to teach me how to live because I WILL see the goodness of the Lord while I am living on this earth.

See you got to get passionate about your future instead of living in your past. You have to demand more for your life and yourself than what you've experienced. As stated before, you are not what you've done. You are not the mistakes you've made. You are not the mistakes you are going to make. You ARE God's son, who has been made in the image and likeness of God, the God who died so that you can live life and live life more abundantly, therefore, if Christ would do that for you knowing that you would fail sometimes, make mistakes, and reject him. You at least should love him enough to love yourself and walk with your head up because he laid down his life for yours.

I don't write this book as a divorcee; I write this book as a STRONG MAN who has experienced a divorce but didn't allow his divorce to define him. Though I started this book as a married man, and am ending it as a divorced one, God still loves me and is allowing me to write this book to show you that you can make it and should love yourself just as much as he does. I wish I could tell you that being a strong man would be easy, but if it was, every man would be one. I Love you man, Stay Blessed!

Practical Daily Steps to help grow your Self-Confidence

1. Affirm yourself daily
2. Dress up when you're feeling your worse
3. Adopt a weekly physical fitness regimen
4. Surround yourself with positive and loving people
5. Develop fun and exciting free-time activities
6. Attend weekly church meetings or services
7. Set Big Goals and pursue them by setting small goals
8. Talk to your accountability partner or a close friend/family member when you are feeling down or discouraged
9. Find ways to serve others who are less fortunate or in need.
10. Pray, fast, Worship, and read the Bible

CHAPTER 8
BOYS OR GIRLS: MY BATTLE WITH HOMOSEXUALITY

1 Corinthians 14: 33(KJV)

For God is not the author of confusion, but of peace, as in all churches of the saints.

As a man, it's hard to admit that you're confused about your sexuality. This is especially true in the African American culture because there's a major divide between the LGTBQ community and the church. Even those who don't attend church weekly are not as accepting of homosexually. So consequently, if a straight man was having homosexual thoughts and was confused about his sexuality, who would he talk to if he needed help? For years, though I've never committed any homosexual act, I was haunted by homosexual thoughts and forced into an area of shame and confusion. I believe this is part of the reason why many strong men fall to homosexuality because, at the introduction of that lifestyle, they had no man to navigate them through that phase of life. They had nobody to confide in that could lovingly guide them and nurture them through this process. This chapter focuses on helping men understand what they're going through and how to overcome thoughts of homosexuality so they may walk in their God-ordained purpose as strong men.

Early Childhood Abuse

I didn't realize what she was doing to me as I laid there pinned to the floor. Excited but confused, restrained, and afraid, I honestly kind of enjoyed it. See, my next-door neighbors' daughter was my babysitter throughout my elementary school summers and used to watch her little brother and I while our mothers were at work. I will never forget how much fun he and I used to have together every day as we played with yo-yo's, dominos, cards, remote control cars, and whatever else we could put our hands on. Life was great until something happened.

At first, I thought it was a game when she used to pin me down and straddle me like a horse while rocking back and forth. I didn't know any better and just went along for the ride because I couldn't get up, heck she was bigger than me. However, the problem came in when I started to like the feeling of her motions and I expected it when in her presence. It was like an adrenaline rush that flowed through my body that I had never felt before and I didn't understand why. At a young age, I was exposed to a lifestyle of perversion.

I would love to say that was the only time I was forced into that type of position, but it wasn't. This happened to me again by other female family members as well. It seemed like this form of touching and seduction was normal, but I later found out that these actions towards me were considered molestation and were wrong. I was inappropriately touched and subdued against my will.

Since I thought this form of touching was normal; I begin to look for the next person to fill in the gap where the other person left off. So, throughout my early years of adolescents and pre-adulthood, I went from girl to girl to girl. Never once seeking a man, but the perverted thoughts followed me consistently. This is not because I wanted to feel the touch of a man, it was because I was chasing the feeling that I was introduced to by my molesters'.

This may seem a bit graphic, but it is the truth and if you have experienced any of what I have expressed in this chapter so far, you may find answers to why you were or are so avid about performing sexual acts or tempted with thoughts of homosexuality.

See the thoughts aren't an indication that you are or will eventually be in a relationship with a man. They are ideas that satan sends us to see if we are weak or vulnerable enough to accept them. As I stated earlier, as far back as elementary school, I can remember having these satanic impulses, but I had the strength to stand against them. Unfortunately, after being mentally and physically attacked this way for so long, many have chosen to live this type of lifestyle. However, homosexual relationships are against the will of God for a person's life. Here are a few scriptures that speak about sexual immorality:

- 1 Corinthians 6: 18 says, "Flee from sexual immorality. All other sins a person commits are outside the body, but whoever sins sexually, sins against their own body" (NIV).
- Galatians 5: 19- 21 says, "The acts of the flesh are obvious: sexual immorality, impurity and debauchery; idolatry and witchcraft; hatred, discord, jealousy, fits of rage, selfish ambition, dissensions, factions and envy; drunkenness, orgies, and the like. I warn you, as I did before, that those who live like this will not inherit the kingdom of God" (NIV).
- 1 Thessalonians 4: 3-5 (ESV) says, "For this is the will of God, your sanctification: that you abstain from sexual immorality; that each one of you know how to control his own body in holiness and honor, not in the passion of lust like the Gentiles who do not know God

Reading these scriptures, I want you to know that it is not your fault. Satan has been after you since you were born with high hopes to destroy the image of God through your life. The devil has been infiltrating your thoughts with sins, temptations, and lusts of the flesh. Check out the list of acts that the flesh desires in Galatians 5:19-21. All these things are fighting for your acceptance from childhood and It's even worse if you are abused sexually or introduced to sex in any way as a child.

Satan knew what he was doing in my life, so he used those closest to me to confuse me and send me on a path of perversion and lustful desires which would hinder my confidence and cause me not to love myself. So, to prove that I wasn't a homosexual, I had more sex with girls and entertained more woman. Instead of being confident in who I was, I worked to prove who I was, and nobody even knew. His lies were so convincing that I was willing to give my body away to prove him wrong.

See, I want to tell you that it is satan's job to lie to you. John 8: 44 says it this way, "... He was a murderer from the beginning, not holding to the truth, for there is no truth in him. When he lies, he speaks his native language, for he is a liar and the father of lies" (NIV). Satan is so afraid of you stepping into your position as a strong man in your house that he was willing to attack you when you were young, vulnerable, and unable to fight for yourself. But I declare to you that you are God's son and you are not who Satan says you are. Whether he is telling you to that you desire men, should give your body away to multiple women, or view children in a perverted manner, you are a strong man who has been set free from all sexual immorality and lustful desires by the power of Jesus' blood that was shed for you and me.

Satan is after Men

Let me tell you something, Satan is after men. He doesn't want you to walk in sonship, have happy sexual marriages, or raise Kingdom-minded kids. He doesn't want you to love yourself, love God, or love others because he knows that a strong man will protect his house if he knows that he is strong. He knows that a strong man of God is one that will fight for the Kingdom of God and seek out souls to be saved. He knows that a strong man of God is one of faith and can speak things that be not as though they are! So, I am telling you right now that if you are facing thoughts of perversion, lust, or homosexuality you can be delivered. See satan inserts this lie into the minds of men because he knows if we walk in homosexuality or follow our lustful passion, we mock God. The Bible does say that Satan is the accuser of the brethren, therefore, when he tricks us into believing his lies, he can go before God and accuse men of not walking in the image God created for us to walk in.

There is a danger when a man doesn't know the truth and relies on the lies of satan. This fact is true for many men and was true for my life because I didn't realize that I was valuable, loved, and wanted. I didn't know I was strong, powerful, and anointed. I didn't know that I had more to offer than what I could provide for people or how I could use my body to please women. I was lost and bound by my ignorance, wherein the enemy took advantage of and led me in his lies. This is why it's so crucial that you search the truth of God's word to see who you are. It's in the word of God that you find your value, worth, and identity and can stand against the wiles of the devil. Here are a few things that God says about you.

- Psalms 1: 1-3- Blessed is the man Who walks not in the counsel of the ungodly, Nor stands in the path of sinners, Nor sits in the seat of the scornful; But his delight is in the law of the Lord, And in His law he meditates day and night. He shall be like a tree Planted by the rivers of water, That brings forth its fruit in its season, Whose leaf also shall not wither; And whatever he does shall prosper.
- 1 Corinthians 11: 7- A man ought not to cover his head, since he is the image and glory of God; but woman is the glory of man.

- 1 Kings 2: 2-3- "I go the way of all the earth; be strong, therefore, and prove yourself a man. 3 And keep the charge of the Lord your God: to walk in His ways, to keep His statutes, His commandments, His judgments, and His testimonies, as it is written in the Law of Moses, that you may prosper in all that you do and wherever you turn;

- Proverbs 21: 22(ESV)- A wise man scales the city of the mighty and brings down the stronghold in which they trust.

What these verses provide is a foundation upon which you can stand and begin your new life outside of the lies of perversion, lust, and homosexuality. The word of God threatens Satan because he knows that once you come to know the truth, the truth shall set you free. So, I ask you right now to write down all the negative things that you have felt about yourself. Write down every lie that satan has told you like; you will never be successful, you will never get married, your marriage will not last, you are a gay, you like men, isn't he cute! Whatever he says, I need you to compare that to the Word of God and begin to declare the Word of God over your life. This will not only free you from this satanic bondage but empower you to walk in the power of God as well.

See though I've always had girlfriends and was married, Satan never stopped talking. It's like he was trying to wear me down to the point that I would stop fighting and take heed to what he had been saying and I want to tell you sir to keep on fighting. No matter what he says or tempts you with, keep on fighting.

The Power of Confession

My greatest deliverance comes from my ability to confess my faults in front of the people that I love and to God. As an ordained evangelist of my church - one that teaches, preaches and serves; I went before them and confessed my feelings and experiences of molestation and proceeding thoughts of homosexuality. I was afraid, nervous, and anxious, but through my confession,

I gained deliverance and freedom from my secret battle. After this, I received much love from my church family and learned that other men had faced or had been through some of the same things.

So, I'm not saying that you have to do this in front of your church, but maybe you have a strong brother that you can talk to. Maybe you have a family member, church leader, Pastor, or community member that you are close too and trust. Share with them your pain and deepest secrets and watch how God is able to free you and empower you to empower others. This is the only way that I'm able to write this chapter to you. It's not easy and every word that I type is proof of my deliverance, but I thank God that I am able to push past my insecurities and share my story with you so that God can work in your life as well.

So, I write this chapter to say that you are not alone, and you are not abnormal. I know you love God, yourself, and your family and these thoughts, experiences, and feelings haunt your manhood and hinder your ability to be strong consistently. But I pray now in the name of Jesus Christ that you're a strong man, one who has been called according to the purpose of God and that you will not submit to homosexuality or thoughts of perversion or lust. You shall stand in the love and power of God and walk in peace. As God delivers you, I pray that you shall have the strength to speak about your experience and help other young boys and men all over the world to be free as well. You are a Strong Man!

You're a World Changer! You're God's son and no weapon formed against you shall prosper, so rise brother, and know that God has been with you all your life. He has always loved you and is not ashamed of you. Even if you have found yourself performing homosexual acts, know that God is your father as well. Know that God will and can heal you from homosexuality if you allow him because he loves you and desires that you walk in his image. No matter how many people have rejected, abandoned, or abused you - God is the one that can heal and restore your footsteps. You are a Man of God, and I speak right now that the Holy Spirit shall begin to work on your behalf and the Word of God prick your heart. I love you brother and know that God does too. #YouAreAStrongMan

CHAPTER 9
FATHERLESSNESS: I WANT MY DADDY

"I am so proud of you"

-Fredrick Vann

There is nothing like hearing your father say, "Good job son." Many sons go days, weeks, and even years without hearing this from their fathers and unfortunately some never do. One of the greatest hindrances of my childhood was not having my father physically in my life and having the opportunity to be in his presence from day-to-day. Though he was not neglecting his responsibilities as a father due to serving in the military, not having the ability to hear his voice and feel his embrace truly hindered me as a young boy. Now, God has restored our relationship and as a grown man, I'm able to share the moments with him that I've always wanted to.

How about you - was your father in your life growing up? If not, how did his absence make you feel or was your father in the home, yet still not the father that you desired? I ask these questions because you will find that the answers to these questions play a role in your self-esteem, confidence, and ability to live life happily and if not addressed, the negative emotions that derive from your relationship with your father can have drastic effects on your life today. Therefore, this chapter focuses on addressing the results of broken father-son relationships and how to be restored from them through the acceptance of God as one's father and Lord of your life.

When is Daddy Coming Home?

As an Army brat, I lived many days wondering when my father would be home. Year after year he was on active duty serving in Iraq, Kuwait, Korea, or Oklahoma while my mother and I settled at Fort Benning in Columbus, GA. My father's absence was okay during the first few years because I was distracted by the many basketball games, school programs, and church events, but after a while, I started to think that maybe my father was never coming home.

This apprehension grew more apparent through middle school and was even more unshakable in high school because it would be during my 9th-grade year that my parents' would get divorced after 20 years of marriage. So, imagine a son who has been desiring for his father to come home after being separated from him for years only for his parents to get divorced. I didn't know what to do. I was angry, upset, confused, and didn't know who to trust. I blamed my mother because I believed it was her fault for running my father away; however, on the other hand, I held my father accountable for not trying hard enough. This view is common for many of us who may have experienced something like this, but my perspective was seen through the lens of disappointment and fueled by the feelings of rejection and abandonment.

Rejection and Abandonment

Rejection- to refuse to accept, consider, submit to, to refuse to hear, receive, obsolete, to cast off.

Abandonment- to leave and never return to (someone who needs protection or help); to give up to the control or influence of another person or agent

Author Edward Kruk Ph. D. writer of the article titled Father Absence, Father Deficit, Father Hunger, writes about the results of absent fathers due to various situations such as divorce by saying, "Whereas parents, in general, are not supported as parents' by our social institutions, divorced fathers, in particular, are devalued, disparaged, and forcefully disengaged from their children's lives. Researchers have found that for children, their results are nothing short of disastrous, along several dimensions:

- Children's diminished self-concept, and compromised physical and emotional security (children consistently report feeling abandoned when their fathers are not involved in their lives, struggling with their emotions and episodic bouts of self-loathing)
- Behavioral problems (fatherless children have more difficulties with social adjustment, and are more likely to report problems with friendships, and manifest behavior problems; many develop a swaggering, intimidating persona to disguise their underlying fears, resentments, anxieties and unhappiness)
- Truancy and poor academic performance (71 percent of high school dropouts are fatherless; fatherless children have more trouble academically, scoring poorly on tests of reading, mathematics, and thinking skills; children from father absent homes are more likely to play truant from school, more likely to be excluded from school, more likely to leave school at age 16, and less likely to attain academic and professional qualifications in adulthood.
- Delinquency and youth crime, including violent crime (85 percent of youth in prison have an absent father; fatherless children are more likely to offend and go to jail as adults)

This information may seem like a lot but whether you are a current father who may be away from your children or a son who has a broken relationship with his father, knowing this information can bring clarity and healing. Understanding the results of an absent father can help a son to understand more of his ways. With this information, I've been able to trace the root of my low self-esteem, lack of courage, timidity, shame, and many inconsistencies. I've also been able to determine the origin of my attention-seeking behavior, need for affection, and search for acceptance in individuals and small groups. See whether you are reading this chapter through the lens of a father, son, or both, know that your presence and love is essential. Your life is important, and God wants to be a part of your life and transform you into the man that he has called you to be.

Hurtful Celebration

During one of my military deployments, my father sent me a picture of himself receiving his Master's Degree...I will never forget that day. I've always known my father to be an educated man and one who reads so for him to be able to accomplish this task was amazing. Excited, I began to email him back my congratulations and I found myself starting to cry, but those tears weren't tears of joy. A deep cry of pain came out of me and my words of encouragement turned to words of disappointment and shame because, at that very moment, I came face to face with the feelings I had oppressed for years. Though I was excited for him, I could no longer run from the hurt inside. So, I began to tell him how I felt about my childhood and the things he'd done; I even told him how I felt about his wife and her children. I apologized for my feelings, but I could no longer hold them in. Although, I was a grown man and on my own, I was still carrying the pains of my childhood.

What about you? Are you holding on to bitterness, resentment, or anger towards your father that you haven't expressed? Have you forgiven your father for the things he has done or hasn't done whether he has apologized or not? Or are you a father who has not forgiven yourself for the mistakes you've made in your child's life and live daily locked in a prison of regret and shame? If you are the son, know that for you to truly be free and happy in your life, you must forgive your father. No matter what he has done or hasn't done, you must forgive him because if you don't, in your efforts to be unlike him, you will subconsciously take on his character traits. However, if you are a father, for you to be free and happy on the inside, or available to reconcile your relationship with your children, you must accept God's forgiveness and forgive yourself. We all make mistakes and find ourselves doing things the wrong way, but we serve a God that is willing and able to forgive us and turn us into a new man free from sin and shame. So, before we go any further please pray this prayer:

Jesus, I love you and thank you for all you've done for me. Thank you for dying for me and rising with all power in your hands. I ask that you forgive me for the wrong I've done and will do and that you will create in me a clean heart and renew in me a right spirit. Lord, you are the God that heals me and draws near to the broken hearted, so please heal my heart from shame, guilt, hatred, anger, low self-esteem, self-condemnation, sadness, and pain. Take away this heart of stone and give me a heart of flesh, in the Name of Jesus Christ, Amen.

The Replacements

So due to my father's obligation to service, my mother did her best to raise and rear me as a young man. You know they say that women can't raise men, but my mama did a pretty good job at it. However, she couldn't do it all on her own. So, she did the best she could to put me around strong men who could show me how to be a man. Thinking back, I don't know if she did this as a scare tactic or not, but she ensured that I had at least one man to look up to and to seek guidance from. One of them was Mr. Cornelius, who served in the U.S. Army with my father but was stationed in the same area my mom and I lived. He was a tall, dark-skinned, hairy, deep-voiced, and big hand man that looked like a giant who had the voice of God. I was afraid of him and anytime I got into trouble, my mother took me to his house.

Mr. Cornelius was a manly man who had a beautiful wife and two daughters who became some of my closest friends. He always talked to me about being the man of the house and what men did and did not do. I learned a lot from him, but mostly I knew not to mess up so I wouldn't have to feel the wrath of his mighty hands. Secondly, there was Uncle Freddie, who wasn't my blood uncle, but he was also a fellow soldier who had served with my father as well. Now he was nicer, and I could always look to him for a smile and some encouragement. We always had fun with him and his family and I knew with them I would be safe.

Thirdly, there was my late Uncle, Samuel Montgomery. Now, Uncle Sam was my second daddy. He lived in Eastaboga, AL with the rest of my family and my mom and I traveled there on a weekly basis. It was only 2 hours and 30 minutes away from our Columbus residence so anytime we had the opportunity to go, we went and I loved it because I knew I would see my grandmother and my Uncle Sam. Uncle Sam was very special to me because he taught me a lot about work ethic, creativity, entrepreneurship, and love. Though he wasn't perfect, there was never a time that he wasn't found cutting someone's grass, driving a tractor-trailer, working in the city, driving a dump truck, lifting lumber, digging ditches, or whatever he could put his hands on. He could work.

I looked up to him so much and wanted to be like him, but things changed. He got caught up into some bad stuff and would eventually be sentenced to jail. I remember the night like it was yesterday when my mother and I found out what happened. Immediately, my mother drove to our local church and we met with our pastor. With my eyes filled with tears, and my mouth lost for words, I could only cry in despair because not only was my Uncle in Jail, but my second father was gone. I wouldn't be able to touch him, love him, or see him like I once did. Time after time I went to visit him through a glass and he would greet me with his same charming smile, but beneath it a deep disappointment because he didn't want me to see him the way I did. However, he still asked about my schooling, girlfriends, life, and told me to take care of my mom.

Eventually, he would get out and life would resume. I was older, but our relationship didn't take a break. I still came down and worked with him. He taught me how to cut grass, edging the lawn, operate a mini crane, etc. I was becoming a man, but as time progressed, his health would decline and he would later pass away in 2019. I had the honor of eulogizing his funeral and expressing who he was to me and how his love changed many. I shared these stories because you never know what little boy may be looking to you for guidance, insight, and inspiration and you don't even know it.

I'm learning now that there are many young boys and men who look up to me - some even call me dad because they're in such a need for a father. I am only 30 years old, but for these teenage boys to look at me in that way is crazy, but honorable to think that as a single man with no kids, that I carry a father like spirit that is inspiring sons to be better. Honestly speaking, I don't know how this became. As you already know, I wasn't raised by my father or had a consistent man in my home, but God somehow made me able to father others as he fathered me. This is important for you to understand because maybe you didn't have a father figure growing up. Maybe you were all on your own but know that God can turn you into a father and use you to change lives if you allow him too. I believe to get to this point; I had to first acknowledge how I felt about my dad and express it. I had to search deep to let go of the resentment and understand who my dad was.

The Other side of the Story:

The Resolution

About a year ago, after a very impactful bible study, I called my father and expressed again how I was feeling. Though I had already expressed how I felt back in 2013, there was still a part of me that was hurting. Please note this because though you may forgive your father or a father figure, you may still experience moments of pain and hurt. So, while on the phone, I expressed how I felt and my father lovingly listened and understood. Little did I know that this would be a breakthrough moment for him as well because he had the opportunity to express how he felt towards me. He was able to explain to me how he was anticipating that conversation and why he worked so hard and chose to be away for the betterment of our family. See from the outside looking in, my father chose to be away from my mother and I because he didn't love us and chose another family over us. But the truth was that he was willing to sacrifice for our long-term success. This conversation truly helped me and brought me much relief as well as my father because it gave us the opportunity to communicate.

See what I didn't know was that my father barely knew his father. They had a very estranged relationship. My father grew up in very meager means and his family was barely able to make ends meet. So, he vowed that his children would never have to live in the projects or 5 to a bedroom like he did, therefore, once he had the opportunity, he joined the military and used it as the vehicle to provide financial support and security for his family.

He told me that he did what he did so I wouldn't have to struggle. He put himself in harm's way so I wouldn't have too. He struggled overseas so I wouldn't have too. Even as a current PTSD survivor, my father understood that his condition is worth it because he can see the man that I am today. As a child, I couldn't understand this, but as a man, I respect him because sometimes you got to do what you got to do, and that was his mindset. Yeah, he could've chosen another route, but I respect and honor his efforts. See, my mother and I were never in lack. He made sure we had anything that we needed, he often called, and showed up when he was able to take leave. He sent me gifts from Korea and overseas and made sure that I understood the history of our black culture. My dad is a King and I wouldn't trade him for the world.

So, if you can, try hard to contact your father and express to him how you feel no matter his response because the conversation is for you. Being able to confront your emotions and express them will work wonders for your self-esteem, take much stress off your heart, and begin your internal healing process. Who knows, maybe you will have the experience I had and be able to rebuild your relationship with your father. If your father is no longer alive or you are unable to contact him, I suggest that you go to God in prayer and that you seek him for complete healing and the ability to forgive your father. If you are a father and unable to reach your son or children, I also suggest that you go to God and seek him for your complete healing and the ability to forgive yourself. There is still time for a resolution and redemption. If you're reading this book, you still have time. So, don't give up, keep your head up, and keep moving forward. You can't change the past, but you can determine the direction of your future.

Lessons Learned

In all of this, I've learned a few things. The first major lesson I've learned is that God is our true father. David expresses this in Psalms 68: 5 who describes God as, "Father to the fatherless, defender of widows— this is God, whose dwelling is holy." (NLT). This truth is so powerful to believe because amid all the hurt and pain you may have experienced, God is your father. He is your provider, your protector, your guide, your leader, your consoler, and your friend. If you allow him, he can be everything that your father wasn't for you and more.

This was the liberating truth that I discovered this year, which allowed me to let go of the residue of my past. God told me that it was meant for my father not to be physically in my life. This may seem harsh, but he explained to me that for me to be the man of God that I am today, God had to raise me and govern my life himself. See God knows all things and doesn't make mistakes, so reevaluate your life because now you may be able to look back and see how God divinely raised you and fathered you without you knowing it. You may be able to see that your life worked out better without your father present. You may be able to see that if your birth father was in your life, you may have picked up on some of his bad habits that would've gotten you into trouble.

I dare you to take an assessment of the good men that God allowed to be in your life, because I mentioned a few of them here but I have many Uncles that took the time to raise me and guide me along the way. I dare you to reach back to them and say thank you for standing in the gap for me. So, thank you for being there when I needed you. Even if he wasn't a family member but possibly a teacher, civic leader, pastor, coach, or mentor. Take some time to reach out to them and say thank you for what they did in your life, because you probably wouldn't be who you are right now without them.

Challenge

1 Peter 5: 2 (NLT)

Care for the flock that God has entrusted to you. Watch over it willingly, not grudgingly—not for what you will get out of it, but because you are eager to serve God. Don't lord it over the people assigned to your care but lead them by your own good example.

When I first started studying this scripture, I looked at it from the perspective of a leader. I saw it as an instruction to Ministry leaders to govern themselves properly and to lead their flock by living a positive example. But now, I view this text through the lens of a man and I believe that every man has the responsibility to shepherd, cover, and lead those around them. It's the job of men to set order, structure, and discipline, also to provide hope, assurance, and believe that all things are possible through Christ. It's time out for us as men to live selfishly, without regard to those around us and the example that we set. It is our time to stand up for what is right and live righteously so that those coming after us can build off the foundation we set. So, I challenge you to take care of the young men and women that are around you. Whether they are your kids, neighbors', communities' kids, nephews, nieces, whoever I challenge you to love them all as if they were your own.

I challenge you to teach them what you do wrong and prepare them to be better. I challenge you to give them the road map to your successes and empower them to surpass you 10 times over. I challenge you to speak into their lives things that they cannot see and declare things that they have never heard. I challenge you to confront their wrongs and wrap them with love after conflict. I challenge you to challenge men who aren't stepping up to the plate and neglecting their responsibilities. I challenge you to push the agenda of fatherhood and help your fellow fathers who are in need. I challenge you to seek help for yourself when you don't have the answer and ultimately seek God for clarity in times of confusion. Ultimately, the life you live is about you and what you do with it, but there are those in the background who are watching you and wishing that they could be just like you.

Out of all you've been through, how did you get to where you are? How did you somehow make it out of your hometown, graduate from high school, go to college, get your GED, start your own business, or start serving in ministry? How did you discover your calling and purpose and begin to help others to walk in theirs? These are all things that God, your father, placed in you and led you to do outside of your control and he wants us to know that he has so much more in store for us. So, I challenge you today: though you may have a natural father, allow God to be your true father and let him govern your life. Accept his unfailing love and purpose for your life and begin to walk in his Image. He created you to walk like him, talk like him, and be like him, and God is the greatest example of a man that we will ever have. So, love him because he first loved you! I love you, Strong Man!

CHAPTER 10
MARRIAGE 101: TERRIFIED OF BEING WITHOUT HER

1 John 4: 19(KJV)

There is no fear in love; but perfect love casteth out fear: because fear hath torment. He that feareth is not made perfect in love.

After being married for almost 7 years I learned that marriage is for grownups. I've learned when to speak and when not to speak. I've learned when to love and when to give space, but most recently I learned that I was terrified of being without my wife. Now I know the word terrified may seem a bit strong but it was my scary reality to face. Though this was shocking for me to discover at the time, it changed my life and my entire perspective about marriage and I know that it will help you as well.

I'm writing this chapter because I believe that there are other men like me who are in relationships out of fear instead of love. You may have started the relationship in love but somewhere along the way that love turned into desperation due to the fear of possible separation. Therefore, this chapter is focusing on rebuilding your love and confidence within yourself so that you won't grow dependent on your spouse and damage the foundation of your relationship with your spouse or with God.

"The best marriages are the ones in which both husband and wife act as if their spouse is far better than they deserved" (MarriageToday, 2013, p. 30). These are powerful words written in the book titled Happy, Happy, Love: Tips & Techniques to refresh your marriage and restore the romance, however, they can be dangerous if a spouse takes them too far. There is a fine line between honoring a spouse and seeing them in an idolized manner and I believe there are many of us who are straddling between the two. Unfortunately, I fell victim to this very mindset and found myself in a situation that was unhealthy for me and my spouse at the time causing damage to both of our lives. Therefore, please, if you don't take the time to read and focus on any other chapter, please take heed to this one because I believe it can truly transform you and prevent you from having to experience things like major heartbreak, trauma, anxiousness, fear, separation, and divorce. Whether you are dating, in a serious relationship, engaged, newly married, been married for a while, or divorced, this chapter is for you.

Let's get started.

If you were to rate the overall wellbeing of your relationship between 1 and 10, what would your number be? There is no wrong or right answer, but please take the time to answer because whether your relationship is at a 10, 5, or 1, they all face problems and tribulations sometimes. For many, the love, fire, passion, excitement, and acts of service that their relationship once possessed has now turned into mere performances because internally they're not happy but they continue to work on their relationship not because they love their partner but because they are afraid to lose them.

Many men are not just cutting the grass, working out, getting new jobs, or cleaning the house because it's their passion, they're doing these things to make themselves more marketable in the eyes of their partner because they are being tormented by their own insecurities. They stress themselves out day and night and beat themselves up over small mistakes so much so, that they leave themselves no room for grace. This is not only a hindrance to their self-confidence but can be a major hindrance to their relationship with God. Brother, if this is you, please know that you no longer have to live this way. You no longer have to live in a prison of insecurity or be tormented by the fear of being alone. If not, your marriage or relationship may be great but please don't underestimate the power of this chapter and apply the truths that are presented in order to fortify yourself and the longevity of your marriage. Let's Continue!

It's the Simple Things!

Why won't she talk to me? Does she even see me? Why doesn't she want to have sex? Do I add value to her life? Is she tolerating me? These are some of the questions that plagued my mind for years that pushed me into the prison of fear and insecurity as it pertained to my marriage. I say to myself that I would've been okay if she would've smiled more, or I would've been okay if she would've asked me about my day, or been interested in my business plans, or even initiated a simple hug or kiss, but is that true? Of course, by her doing those things more often it would've helped me feel more secure in our relationship but should it have been the source of my security? See I believe every man deserves to be treated like a king. Every man wants their girl to love on them and make them feel special. Every man wants their girl to tell them how great they are. Every man wants to be waited on but what happens if your boo, girlfriend, or wife doesn't do it?

Another question is, what if your wife doesn't know how to show love because growing up she never received love and affection either? See my ex-wife was raised without a father present in her life and a mother who was not stable. Though she had other brothers and sisters, she was forced to fend for herself and developed a very hard exterior in order to protect herself. This protective covering made her very hard to love at times and difficult for her to love others because of her lack of trust for people. Therefore, I'm speaking up for those women and want to let you know that if you are married to or dating a young lady like this that you have a jewel and she is worth it. Though it will be tough at times, God has the ability to change her and make her a loving soul if she submits to him.

As stated earlier, I say to myself that I would've been more secure if she would've done more but that isn't the whole truth because the truth is that I came into my marriage with baggage and insecurities. I didn't realize the magnitude of them at the time because I was so excited to have a wife and to be starting a new life. See, I was able to hide in the newlywed state and forsake having to deal with my internal issues. Not only was I able to hide them, I was also in and out to sea due to my active duty service in the military, so our first year of marriage we were apart for 266 days.

However, I needed to be healed because there were some emotional wounds that I had neglected to tend to and ignored them by going to school, joining the navy, going to church, working out, starting a business, and getting married. It was easy for me to be confident when I was married to a 5'9" basketball player who possessed two degrees, served God, walked in confidence, extroverted, and could take care of herself. It was easy for me to pose as a strong man because my wife was strong however; when I began to feel that she was ready to leave I began to panic and didn't know what to do. I didn't tell anyone because I was prideful but deep down on the inside I dreaded the thought of her leaving me alone.

So one day while attending a service to support a brother in ministry, he began to preach about separating oneself from people who mean you no good. Then he began to speak about cutting people off and getting rid of dead weight and at the very moment, standing right beside my wife, a force of terror derived from within and my heart began to beat frantically. It was at that moment that I realized that something was wrong and I needed God's help. I realized that I had a deep seeded fear that my wife would leave. So I immediately began to pray and go before the altar to worship and praise God because I knew that those feelings were wrong. I knew that I had allowed these feelings to go on for too long and I was now positioning my wife to be an idol instead of my spouse. I say this because I had gotten to the point that I was more afraid of her opinion than God's. I was more afraid of being without her than being without God. So it was at that point that I readjusted myself, gave my life back to God, and started a new path.

Now this process wasn't easy because even after that night my wife and I still had problems. We had countless conversations about her unhappiness and lack of motivation within our marriage. We talked about my inconsistencies and downfalls. She would also later confess that she was no longer in love with me and desired to move out and did!

I don't know how to properly explain how I felt but these conversations and her desire to separate were dreadful yet confirmed the truth that I was afraid of. I share these personal things with you in order for you to see the results of uncommunicated feelings. Around our 3rd year of marriage I began to feel the separation occur but I was afraid to acknowledge it. I could tell that something was different but I was too afraid to confront it because if my feelings were true, I would have to face yet another rejection and abandonment. Deep down, even as a husband, preacher, teacher, leader, and adult, I still struggled with the rejection and abandonment that occurred from my parents as a child. Therefore, subconsciously, I became a yes man and strived for perfection not because I was doing it out of pure passion and desire but because I was striving to prevent someone from leaving me again.

I don't know if you have ever felt these types of emotions towards your friends, family, girlfriend, or spouse, but if you do, first be honest about how you feel and talk to God. Tell him about your hurt, pain, and feelings of rejection and allow him to mend your heart. Along with this, ask him to give you the courage to speak up about how you feel and the grace to take whatever response you receive. One thing that I often practiced in my marriage was praying for a conversation that I would have with my spouse later on in the day. If I knew that the topics that were to be discussed were tough or uncomfortable, I asked God to help me communicate and for his spirit to be in the midst of it. Brother, I know it is hard to communicate sometimes but if you do not get these emotions off of your chest, you will be tormented daily and grow a sense of resentment towards the one you love and begin to criticize everything that they do.

Not only will you begin to grow resentment towards them, you will also begin to grow a deep resentment and disappointment for yourself because you know what to do but you are too afraid to do it. I did this for years! I would preach, teach, and counsel other people, but I was afraid to speak myself. I was afraid of what I might hear or what she might say to the point that I compromised living a life of prosperity, freedom, and love to live a life of shame, disappointment, and resentment. It got so bad that I lost myself! I lost Robert and couldn't find him. Actually, I stopped looking for him and was comfortable being miserable and overlooked.

I was comfortable surviving instead of living and I want to prevent you from doing the same. Sir, you are a King amongst men! You are a Son of God, who was created in the image of God and you are worth being loved. Your thoughts, opinions, and feelings matter and you can speak. You have authority and no weapon formed against you shall prosper. I Command right now in the Name of Jesus Christ that you shall be strengthened in the inner man and you shall speak. You Shall live and not die and you shall live out your ordained purpose.

There is no Fear in Love

Reading this chapter so far, you might have begun to notice a recurring theme. In a lot of situations that I mentioned before fear was noted. Fear had such a major grip on me that I didn't have the strength to break out of it alone, but I did, and you can too through the power of God and the Love of Jesus Christ. 1 John 4: 18(NLT) says, "Such love has no fear, because perfect love expels all fear. If we are afraid, it is for fear of punishment, and this shows that we have not fully experienced his perfect love." First, let's start off by recognizing that there is no fear in love. If you are currently in a relationship and you are troubled with fear or anxiousness, that's not love.

If you are constantly worrying about being abandoned or rejected that's not love. If you are unable to rest or relax in the presence of your spouse due to the overwhelming desire to be perfect, that's not love and honestly, it is not healthy. During our marriage I had many panic attacks within because I was warring with my faith and my flesh daily on behalf of my marriage. I couldn't even stand being with my wife alone because I was tormented by the feeling of being inadequate. Therefore, if you are in a relationship where you feel trapped rather than free, take a step back and assess why you may be feeling this way and how to get rid of it.

Secondly, I would like to point out the distinction that John presents by describing love as being "perfect!" This places a whole new meaning on love and causes one to wonder where this love comes from, and to answer the question; this love can only come from God! See perfect love doesn't require anything. God's perfect love doesn't require us to give him anything back for it, or to be perfect, or to love him perfectly. God's perfect love is constant, eternal, and established. It has no ending and can't be tainted. God's love for us is so perfect that he doesn't take it away from us when we do wrong, or leave him, or sin, God's love actually intensifies and desires us the most during our broken times. Therefore, place your anxieties, fears, and concerns before God and allow him to heal your heart from every hurt, pain, rejection, and abandonment you've faced because he desires to fill you with his perfect love and establish you on a firm foundation which is his Son, Jesus Christ.

Thirdly, know that as you allow God to fill you with his perfected love, He himself will deal with and deliver you from your fears. He will mend your heart and change your mind. He will give you a new vision for yourself and teach you how to love yourself. As he is doing this, you will begin to develop a new vision for your partner and your relationship and begin to live the life that God has ordained for you to live. As you are doing this, pray that God does the same in your partner. If you notice that she may be dealing with the same things, love on her and trust God in the process. God has a way of mending the hearts of his people through the perfected love that is demonstrated through others so allow God to work through you on her behalf.

Women will never understand the amount of pressure it is to be a good man. They will never understand how much we actually desire to be great and perfect and how much we beat ourselves up when we mess up. However, in the midst of these things, don't let this pressure and desire for perfection kill you. Don't let your fears box you into a corner for one more day because what you are fearing may not even be real. Let me tell you! My ex-wife never required me to be perfect; I came into the marriage thinking that I needed to be in order to cover up my insecurities. Listen bro, I don't care how jacked up you think you are, you will never reach perfection. You will never be fully delivered, fully pure, fully perfected, or squared away; actually, God designed us to be imperfect. The bible says that we were born into sin and shaped in iniquity and it also says that all the days of a man are filled with trouble. Therefore, your seek for perfection will be endless and unfulfilling until you learn how to love yourself as you are.

Concerning this very topic, I asked women all over Facebook to answer the following question:

Do you find it appealing for a man to desire to be "perfect" for you?

Read what a few of our sisters had to say:

"No one is able to be "Perfect". His desire to be perfect would mean a prideful man and again may lead to undefined insecurities as well as an expectation of perfection from me" - Anonymous Writer

"No, I don't find it appealing for a man to have a desire to be perfect for me. We all have flaws and to me that's what makes my hubby perfect because he's not trying to be perfect, he is being himself" - Anonymous Writer

"NO I DO NOT FIND IT APPEALING FOR A MAN TO BE PERFECT! As a woman I need to know your weaknesses so i will know how to cover you. Don't pretend to be whole in order to please me because I may hit a spot that's still unhealed and open, now we have unnecessary issues and a breakdown in our relationship because of the mask you are wearing" - Anonymous Writer

"This question is a little rough for me as i myself struggle with being a perfectionist. Nothing about trying to be perfect is "appealing" simply because you are left with a lack of authenticity and that's in all aspects. This usually leads to having an IMAGE but no substance and the idea of being with someone for image is a disgusting one. Just love me. Fully and authentically. That's what's appealing" - Anonymous Writer

"I love a man who's desire is to make happy but to be perfect? No. The best thing you can do for me is strive to be the best Man of God you can be and everything else will fall into place. Just love the raw unadulterated me unconditionally. To me… that's enough" - Anonymous Writer

"I have no problem with a man desiring to be perfect for the woman he loves. It says to me, that he really loves me and want to please me at any cost." - Anonymous Writer

These are some powerful words from women from all different walks of life that brings a lot of perspective to the topic of men striving to be perfect. You may be wondering why I am focusing so much on this topic, well it's because I spent years trying to achieve it and it cost me my sanity, health, and marriage, and I know there are other men who are in this cycle as well. Another reason why I placed their words in this book is for us to get the inside scoop of how women really feel about us. To be honest with you bro, it's currently 8: 55p.m on April 01, 2019, and I just texted my ex-wife saying thanks for respecting and loving me though I was internally unhealthy. I shared with her that I was fighting me so much that I had no time to fight for our family and it is because of that, that she was uncovered and left to fend for herself. Therefore, please be careful and trust that if you are in a relationship or married to someone, that they love you for who you are and not who you are trying to be. It is really selfish for us as men or women to not trust someone because we don't believe they accept us even when they have taken a vow of commitment. So be careful, be wise, and be confident.

How can we fix the desire to be perfect?

1. Understand that no one is perfect but God

a. Romans 3: 23(NLT)- For everyone has sinned;

we all fall short of God's glorious standard.

2. Trust in the God in the people that are in your circle

a. Psalms 118: 8(NLT)- It is better to take refuge in the Lord than to trust in people.

b. Proverbs 3: 5(NLT)- Trust in the Lord with all your heart; do not depend on your own understanding.

3. Search your heart for insecurities and give them to God

a. Matthew 11: 28(NLT)- Then Jesus said, "Come to me, all of you who are weary and carry heavy burdens, and I will give you rest.

4. Walk in the power and the Image that God created you to Walk in

a. Genesis 1: 27(NLT)- So God created human beings in his own image. In the image of God he created them; male and female he created them.

To sum all of this up, Men, we are one of God's most beautiful creations. Our value cannot be numbered and our strength cannot be matched. Because we have been made in the image and the likeness of God, we have authority and access heavenly resources at any time. Because we have a powerful makeup and divine connection with God, we're going to face hardships, challenges, and negativity on a daily basis but you have to fight back. You have to fight for yourself, your relationship, marriage, family, church, and community because if you're not healthy, you won't be able to effectively influence the people around you. Therefore, do not forget; it's not what you do that makes you great, it's who you are that makes you great. And who you are is who your friend, girlfriend, fiancé, or spouse wants you to be the most. So be uniquely you and watch how your love for yourself and others grows at an exponential rate. God Bless! Love ya Man!

10 Things that Women really want in a Strong Man

1. A Man who is confident and Secure with himself

2. A Man who walks in authority

3. A Man who can say "No"

4. A Man who desires to be his best Self

5. A Man who is Authentic

6. A Man with a backbone who can check and challenge their partner

7. A man who desires to make his partner happy

8. A man who can love his partner no matter what

9. A man who can be vulnerable and show weakness

10. A Man who Loves God more than his spouse

CHAPTER 11

MOMMY OR DADDY: THE TRIALS OF A SON OF DIVORCED PARENTS

1 Samuel 1: 27-28(NLT)

"I asked the LORD to give me this boy, and he has granted my request. 28 Now I am giving him to the LORD, and he will belong to the LORD his whole life."
And they[a] worshiped the LORD there.

There is nothing like a hug from a Mama! My mother is simply the greatest, though she got on my nerves at times and stressed me out, I have now come to appreciate her love and support because she did the best she could to provide for me and for that I am grateful. Though this is my current perspective of her, it wasn't always that way. There were times that I was angry, upset, and resentful towards her. These feelings stemmed from my father not being in the home and them later getting divorced after 20 years of marriage, I placed all of the blame of him not being there for her. However, throughout life I've learned that as men we need our fathers to cultivate our masculine identity but our mothers are also equally important towards cultivating our emotional and psychological health. Therefore, in this chapter I will utilize my relationship with my mother to discuss the importance of a mother-son relationship and the effects it has on a son, while providing guidance on how to bring reconciliation to a broken or non-existent one. Let's Get it!

During my research I came upon an article on www.telegram.com written by Kate Stone Lombardi titled 5 reasons the mother-son relationship is so important and found these interesting facts:

1) Baby boys who do not have secure attachments with their mothers go on to have behavioral problems later in life. Studies reveal that boys who do not bond securely with their mothers in the infant years act much more hostile, destructive and aggressive later in life. A close bond with their moms when boys were young helped prevent delinquency when they were older.

2) Boys who are close to their mothers perform better in school. Mothers often nurture emotional intelligence in their sons, teaching them to recognize and express their own feelings and to be more attuned to the feelings of others. These boys not only become more articulate--which helps them with reading and writing skills, but also have better self-control in the classroom.

3) A close mother-son relationship is good for a boy's mental health. A study presented at the American Psychological Association showed that boys who are close to their mothers tend not to buy into hyper-masculine stereotypes. They don't believe, for instance, that you have to always act tough, go at it alone or fight to prove your manhood every time you are challenged. These boys remained more emotionally open. Not only did they have better friendships, but also less anxiety and depression than their more macho peers.

After reading these facts were you able to relate? Were you able to see how your relationship with your mother or lack of, affected you as a teen or adult? For me, I was able to trace my successes and failures back to moments in my past and I want to share a few of them with you.

Why is she so loud?

I will never forget the days when my mother used to be the loudest soul in the crowd of every one of my basketball games, band competitions, and chess matches. Yes, chess matches, lol. I mean you could hear her over everybody. Her voice rang out like an ambulance coming through a crowd of cars and there was no one who could stop it. You knew when Ms. Vann was in the building and for so long I was embarrassed by it. I was embarrassed by her constant attendance and activeness during my games and would put my head down as soon as she got riled up. I was ashamed but unaware that it was those moments that would mold me to be the man that I am today.

My mother was the first person to encourage me and the first person to build me up. She ensured that before and after I played in a game, band recital, or chess competition that I knew I was great and not a failure. My mother is the greatest. Even until this day I receive at least two calls a week with a voicemail that states, "I just wanted to hear your voice." Though I still act like I don't like them at times, I look forward to her calls and get upset when she doesn't. I'm so double-minded, lol, but the principle here is that my mother made sure that she molded me into the best man that I could be and allowed God to do the rest just like Samuel's mother in 1 Samuel chapter 1.

1 Samuel 1: 27:28(NLT)

27 I prayed for this child, and the LORD has granted me what I asked of him. 28 So now I give him to the LORD. For his whole life he will be given over to the LORD." And he worshiped the LORD there.

Here in this passage we find a young woman named Hannah who was once barren and unable to have kids. Hannah was often ridiculed and embarrassed about her condition which led her to pray to God and ask him for a child. So

God granted her request and she promised God that if he gave her a son, she would give him back to him after the son was weaned and that is exactly what she did. This brings us to 1 Samuel chapter 1: 27-28 where she gives her son, Samuel, back to God and commits him to his care. This seems like the ideal way that a mother should care for her son but not all do that. So I want to talk about the time between Samuel's birth and when he was given to God. I want to address this time because many men feel that they were dropped by their mothers and maybe you do as well. Maybe you feel like your mother mishandled you growing up and it affected your ability to see yourself as a man and walk in the authority of God but I declare that you can and you will.

There have been only a few times in my life that I felt like my mother dropped me. The first major one was when my parents got divorced after being married for 20 years during my 9th grade year in high school. I understand now that it was not totally her fault but because my father was away and she was the parent that was raising me, as a child I could only assume that it was due to her that he would leave me. So internally and over time, I grew a sense of bitterness and resentment towards her. As a young boy I could only assume that she ran my father off. The only thing that I could see was that she was there, my father was gone, and he would never be back, and it was all her fault. I was confused, hurt, and angry.

Though she would try to communicate to me and worked hard to provide a comfortable life for me, my perspective was already altered and perverted. So when she would have male friends over or talk to any man that was not my father I would get angry. I would be so upset with her because I felt like not only is my father gone but she was already moving on to other people and forsaking how I felt. Though there were only 2 or 3 out of my 29 years of life, I felt that she no longer cared about me and had moved on to bigger and better things.

I understand now that this was not the case and it wasn't her intention but as son's, especially, those of us who didn't have fathers or constant father figures growing up, our emotions were everywhere which made us very vulnerable and unstable. I share this because maybe you have experienced something like this in your life and still foster some bitterness or resentment towards your mother or mother figure and I want you to know that you can be healed and set free. I encourage you to pray and take the time to communicate to your mother or mother figure on how you feel and allow God to begin your healing process. If your mother is no longer alive, the bible tells us in Matthew 11: 28-29(NLT), "Then Jesus said, "Come to me, all of you who are weary and carry heavy burdens, and I will give you rest. 29 Take my yoke upon you. Let me teach you, because I am humble and gentle at heart, and you will find rest for your souls." God wants you to be healed and free from the bondage of your past and if you allow him, he can do that right now.

Get up boy, It's Time For Church!

Every Sunday morning my mother and I had a breakfast routine. We would either go to Hardee's or a buffet called Shoney's. Shoney's was the best. We went there so much that the waitresses would sit us at our usual table and admire our relationship. They would speak about how close we were and how they wish they could do that with their kids. After eating breakfast, we would head to church and she would make me cut the music off as soon as we got into the church parking lot. I didn't realize what she was doing then but now I realize that she was striving to show me how to respect God and his house.

While at church you would find us both being active and apart of multiple things. I often played the drums, sung in the youth choir, or lit the acolyte candles and my mother would be found singing and giving God praise in the St. Mary's Road United Methodist Church Adult choir. When my mother opened her mouth to sing, I would sit there in amazement and fill chills all over my body. She ensured that I listened to the sermon, respected God's house, and prayed; but most importantly, she made sure that I understood how important it was for me to have a personal relationship with God. She trained me up in the way that I needed to go and when I strayed, I knew exactly what to come back to.

This is the way in which my mother raised me, but how did your mother raise you? Did she ensure that you had a relationship with God? Did she ensure that you were safe, fed, and well nourished, or was your mother like Rebecca, Jacob's mother? Rebecca's name in Hebrew means ensnarer, therefore, Jacob whose name means supplanter, heel holder, trickster only became the product of what his mother fed him. This is why it is very important for mothers to understand the significance of what they feed their kids whether it is physically, emotionally, or spiritually. Their voice and opinion is so important to us that we desire to hear their approval and feel their embrace but when a son doesn't get that, there can be major effects. Has your mother ever said, "You are just like your daddy?" Or has she ever said, "You ain't gone never be nothing, you're going to end up just like your daddy, or called you stupid, or dumb?"

See other people can say these things to a son and have no effect on him, but for a mother, the one that birthed him to say these things is hurtful and can be very detrimental in the development of that son's life.

So I ask you, what has your mother said that has positively or negatively affected you? I know my mother always told me that I was special and the best kid in the world. She often encouraged me to try new things, pushed me to be great, never talked down to me negatively, or spoke to me in a derogatory manner. However, after being told that I was just like my father I subconsciously became him. She often said that he loved women and was a flirt and honestly I did too. I would talk to multiple girls at one time and when she would question me about my actions I would say, "Mama, we're just friends." After her comparing me to my father and hearing it so much while living in a house without him, I began to resent him when he was away and praise him when we were together. I would leave my mother at a drop of a dime just to be with my father. Even during my senior year of high school and after graduation I told my mother that I wanted to move out and go live with my father. By this time my father had retired from the Army and was stationed in Atlanta with his new family and I was willing to drop everything just to be with him. I figured life would be better with him and even at the age of 18 I still fostered a bit of resentment towards my mother.

Still hadn't Forgiven my Mother

Needless to say, I decided not to move to Atlanta with him and went on to college in Fairfield, AL to attend the great Miles College. I attended there for a semester, then transferred to Columbus Technical College earning three Certificates in Residential Carpentry, only later to join the United States Navy and get stationed in Norfolk, VA. This move provided freedom and independence that I never had before. I was out of my mother's house and on my own. Shoot, I was finally a GROWN MAN! Nobody could tell me anything. I met a young lady in boot camp who later became my girlfriend and after a year we were planning marriage. It was surely meant to be, but we later broke up and God connected me with a friend from home who eventually became my wife. We got married in January of 2012 and things were going great; until...

After a few years of marriage, navy sea tours, ministry, school, jobs, and responsibilities, the honeymoon phase was over and our real colors were starting to emerge. In the midst of all of my naval accomplishments, ministry development, and outside success, there was still a deep seated hurt that resided in my heart towards my mother that affected my self-esteem and the way I viewed my wife. I didn't realize it but I viewed myself as less than and was insecure because of the brokenness from my childhood. So in order to heal from it I called my mother to talk about it and apologized. We spoke through our differences and I was able to let go all of the baggage from my childhood.

Now I must say, this conversation was great but as time progressed and the more I grew, the more I learned that there was still more deep seated hurt within my heart. Therefore, I had to call again, and again, and again, until I was able to be free completely. I share this because I don't want you to think that all of your problems can go away simply by having one conversation. God has a way of delivering us in phases, and the more we grow the more he shows us to confront and once we do, we are able to get free and continue living our lives.

After this, I found myself talking to my mother more about her faith, teaching her about prayer, and other things concerning Christianity and it made me feel really good. By this time I was an ordained minister and I was now giving back to my mother what she had instilled in me. I write this to you because maybe God wants to heal you in order for you to bring forth healing in your mother's life. It's funny how God uses me to speak into my mother's life just as if I was her pastor. Think about this: My mother raised me in the church, taught me how to pray, read the bible, and to love others, but now that I'm older, I am giving her everything she gave me back. So let me ask you this, is it worth holding on to the pain, hurt, stress, anger, or resentment if you have the opportunity to make your mother better? Don't let what you feel destroy who you are and what you can become because somebody and maybe even your mother needs you.

Divorce???? What does that mean??

Amy Morin, author of the article titled Psychological Effects of Divorce on Children: Take steps to help Kids bounce back writes about this by saying, "As you might expect, research has found that kids struggle the most during the first year or two after the divorce. Kids are likely to experience distress, anger, anxiety, and disbelief. But many kids seem to bounce back. They get used to changes in their daily routines and they grow comfortable with their living arrangements. Others, however, never really seem to go back to "normal." This small percentage of children may experience ongoing—possibly even lifelong—problems after their parents' divorce"

(https://www.verywellfamily.com/psychological-effects-of-divorce-on-kids-4140170). She later goes on to write:

Divorce creates emotional turmoil for the entire family, but for kids, the situation can be quite scary, confusing, and frustrating:

- Young children often struggle to understand why they must go between two homes. They may worry that if their parents can stop loving one another that someday, their parents may stop loving them.

- Grade school children may worry that the divorce is their fault. They may fear they misbehaved or they may assume they did something wrong.

- Teenagers may become quite angry about a divorce and the changes it creates. They may blame one parent for the dissolution of the marriage or they may resent one or both parents for the upheaval in the family.

These are important but compelling facts to consider because I never knew how much growing up in a divorced home affected me. I never knew that a lot of my problems stemmed from the brokenness in my home. If you are someone who has been exposed to divorce in your home and find yourself still broken or resentful, I urge you to talk to your parents, God, or a professional that can walk you through your experience and lead you to a place of resolve. I myself have done all three and I'm an advocate for counseling or therapy because being exposed to divorce is not a joke as a child or teenager. Amy Morin goes on to say this:

- Divorce usually means children lose daily contact with one parent—most often fathers. Decreased contact affects the parent-child bond and researchers have found many children feel less close to their fathers after divorce.

- Divorce also affects a child's relationship with the custodial parent—most often mothers. Primary caregivers often report higher levels of stress associated with single parenting. Studies show mothers are often less supportive and less affectionate after divorce. Additionally, research indicates their discipline becomes less consistent and less effective.

- For a slim minority of children, the psychological effects of divorce may be long-lasting. Some studies have linked parental divorce to increased mental health problems, substance use issues, and psychiatric hospitalizations during adulthood.

- Many studies, including one study in the Journal of Family Psychology, provide evidence that parental divorce could be related to less success in young adulthood in terms of education, work, and romantic relationships. Adults who experienced divorce in childhood tend to have lower educational and occupational attainment and more employment and economic problems.

- Adults who experienced divorce during childhood may also have more relationship difficulties. Divorce rates are higher for people whose parents were divorced.

All of this is important to truly digest, evaluate, and retain because it is no wonder that the divorce rate is going up every year. For one, those who were exposed to divorce are at a higher risk of getting divorced themselves and secondly, the devil loves division. He loves to divide and conquer, and he especially loves to divide families, because if he can divide a family he can possibly destroy the parents and the children who are involved. To prove this, I got divorced after 7 years of marriage in 2018. This was one of the hardest times of my life. One of the lowest places I've ever been in, but as I look back at it now, I remember thinking that I will never end up like my parents. I said that because I was so hurt by the experience that I tried my best to be a perfect husband to prevent divorce, not knowing that perfection is not reality and caused more of a burden on me and my marriage than good. I had no peace in my marriage because i was constantly running from "what if". I was constantly afraid of repeating the cycle. I was constantly fearing the ultimate end, instead of having authority over it and declaring that it wouldn't be.

Bro, please listen to me. If you have been exposed to divorce in your childhood and are currently in a serious relationship, engaged, or married please take in this information because it can save your relationship. Now, check it out. The bible tells us that he has not given us the spirit of fear, but of power, love, and a sound mind. This means that if we are experiencing fear in any area of our lives, it is not from God, it's from ourselves or Satan. Either we are over thinking a situation and making ourselves anxious, or satan is striving to fill you with fear to keep you from pursuing your purpose; either way, fear is not from God. With that in mind, You can NOT defeat something you FEAR!! If you don't remember anything else in this book remember this: You Can NOT Defeat something You FEAR! I say this now because I realize that because I feared divorce, the cycle of divorce had access to my life. I was so afraid of it that I tried to become something I was not in order to attain something I wanted, and anytime you try to change who you are to keep something that you desire you will never keep it.

Anytime you change who you are to ensure that you're successful, you will always find defeat. God created marriage for two whole beings to come together and use what they have to demonstrate his glory, but if one of them comes into the marriage as a form of someone else, the blessings that was supposed to be over the marriage is no longer available because it was only pronounced to the original image of the two. What am I saying, God created us in his image. He created us to look like him, walk like him, talk like him, serve like him, love like him, create like him. We all have our own unique way of doing it and God blesses our uniqueness.

Look at the disciples of Jesus in the New Testament. Out of the 12, there was Matthew, Mark, Luke, and John, the first four writers of the New Testament. They were all writers and disciples of Jesus, whose books are in the bible recollecting the life of Jesus, but they are all written from four different perspectives. They are all writing about the same person around the same time and the same experiences, but they are all different in their own unique ways. Because of this, they were all blessed and we are now able to learn from what they wrote. This same concept of being blessed for walking in the image that God still applies in our individual lives and our relationships. Therefore, if you are in a relationship and afraid to be who God has called you to be in order to try to save it, it will not work and will end because you are trying to save it instead of allowing God to do it himself.

So I tell you this, take authority over your life, be honest about how you feel, communicate your emotions, and allow God to heal you. If I would've known the effect my parents' divorce would've had on me years ago, I would've spoken to my mother and sought help, but honestly, my heart wasn't a priority. I believe this is one of our hardest struggles as men because we are used to working to provide on the outside but we are not comfortable dealing with how we feel on the inside. We know how to work for money, but we don't know how to submit for healing. We know how to have sex for pleasure, but we don't know to kneel for worship.

Therefore, if you can identify with me and see how you were affected by divorce as a child, or may be separated or in the midst of the divorce process, or are already divorced. If you have children, seek God for direction and learn ways to help your children to cope with the new life changes. As I stated before, I didn't like my mom not because she was a bad mom but because I felt bad about myself and if you feel the same way know that God loves you and wants the best for you no matter what. I don't care if you have been divorced, God still loves you, and he still cares and has a plan for your life. Ask him for forgiveness, repent; learn from your mistakes and move forward because there is so much more life to live. I love you man!

Below are some ways that Amy Morin suggest that parents can help children cope with the divorce process:

Parents play a major role in how children adjust to a divorce. Here are some strategies that can reduce the psychological toll divorce has on children:

- Co-parent peacefully. Intense conflict between parents has been shown to increase children's distress. Overt hostility, such as screaming and threatening one another has been linked to behavior problems in children. But minor tension may also increase a child's distress. If you struggle to co-parent with your ex-spouse, seek professional help.
- Don't put kids in the middle. Asking kids to choose which parent they like best or giving them messages to give to other parents isn't appropriate. Kids who find themselves caught in the middle are more likely to experience depression and anxiety.

- Maintain a healthy relationship with your child. Positive communication, parental warmth, and low levels of conflict may help children adjust to divorce better. A healthy parent-child relationship has been shown to help kids develop higher self-esteem and better academic performance following divorce.

- Use consistent discipline. Establish age-appropriate rules and follow through with consequences when necessary. Studies show effective discipline after divorce reduces delinquency and improves academic performance.

- Monitor adolescents closely. When parents pay close attention to what teens are doing and who they spend their time with, adolescents are less likely to exhibit behavior problems following a divorce. That means a reduced chance of using substances and fewer academic problems.

- Empower your child. Kids who doubt their ability to deal with the changes and those who see themselves as helpless victims are more likely to experience mental health problems. Teach your child that although dealing with divorce is difficult, he has the mental strength to handle it.

- Teach specific coping skills. Kids with active coping strategies, like problem-solving skills and cognitive restructuring skills, adapt better to divorce. Teach your child how to manage his thoughts, feelings, and behaviors in a healthy way.

- Help your child feel safe and secure. Fear of abandonment and concerns about the future can cause a lot of anxiety. But helping your child feel loved, safe, and secure can reduce the risk of mental health problems.

- Attend a parent education program. There are many programs available to help reduce the impact divorce has on kids. Parents are taught co-parenting skills and strategies for helping kids cope with the adjustments.

- Seek professional help for yourself. Reducing your stress level can be instrumental in helping your child. Practice self-care and consider talk therapy or other resources to help you adjust to the changes in your family

ROBERT B. VANN

CHAPTER 12
A MAN WITH A VISION

Proverbs 29: 18

Where there is no vision, the people perish: but he that keepeth the law, happy is he.

There is nothing more powerful than a man with a vision and one of the most powerful examples is Jesus Christ. Jesus Christ is a man that was dedicated to his vision no matter who supported him or not. He was a man who knew who he was and wasn't willing to change himself for anyone. His vision brought him so much confidence that he was willing to die for what he believed. Comparatively, like Jesus, other men carried world-changing legacies like Martin Luther King Jr., Gandhi, Barack Obama, Thomas Jefferson, Abraham Lincoln, Booker T. Washington, Albert Einstein, and the Wright Brothers. These men were sure of their dreams, resolute in their beliefs, unmovable towards their mission, and submitted themselves to their vision for the enhancement of those around them. I present these men to let you know that not only do you possess the same world-changing power, but you can even surpass them and have an impact on your area of influence and the world through the manifestation of your vision through faith. Let's begin.

"Sight is what your eyes produce. Vision is what your heart produces. Never let what you see affect your vision."- Shandren Reddy

Introduction

Living life without a vision is dangerous. A vision gives us hope and a reason to live; however, living without hope is not living; it is merely surviving. Have you ever seen the show Survivor? On this show, contestants must go through significant trials, tribulations, and tests to win a prize worth one million dollars. The money wasn't guaranteed and to win it, the contestants were challenged to survive based on their level of survival skills. Throughout these daily challenges to win the ultimate prize and validate their success, some were unable to complete the challenges and were thrown out of the game with nothing.

Now have you ever felt this way? Have you ever felt that your life was filled with trials and tests that you found no hope for tomorrow? Well, there is hope, because God wants to reveal his plans for your life that's filled with happiness, fulfillment, and success. God didn't create us to survive based on how we handle life's various challenges; he called us to live a life far beyond our expectations and imaginations. John 10: 10(NLT) says. "The thief's purpose is to steal and kill and destroy. My purpose is to give them a rich and satisfying life." Therefore, in this chapter, we're going to be discussing what a vision is and what life is without one. We'll also discuss the value of a vision and how important it is to fight for it. Concluding with the steps to complete a vision and why the devil doesn't want that to happen.

What is a Vision?

- Vision- something that you see or dream especially as part of a religious or supernatural experience
- Vision- oracle, dream, divine communication

Life without a Vision!

When I was in high school, I always wanted to fit in. I wanted to be a part of the popular group, nerd group, athletic group, etc., it didn't matter who it was; I just wanted to be accepted, lol. So, I started doing the things they did; I changed the way I dressed, I changed the way I walked, and I changed the way I talked. I wasn't satisfied with my vision and decided to adopt someone else's. This is a bad place to be in life because God has called each one of us to be different, set apart, and unique in our own way. However, if we cast away the vision that God has for us to pick up someone else's, we lose our ability to succeed and fulfill our own destiny.

In 1 Kings chapter 1, there is a story about two brothers named Solomon and Adonijah. Solomon was destined to be king of Israel and his brother Adonijah didn't like that. So, Adonijah gathered a group of people, leaders, and an army and began to declare himself to be king without his father's permission. Adonijah was out of order and didn't have the right or authority to give himself that title. Let me ask you this: How many times have you deemed yourself as something that God has not called you to be? How many times have you deemed yourself as ugly, fat, incapable, dumb, unworthy, unable, insufficient, or unreliable? Well, Proverbs 28: 19 (KJV) says, "Where there is no vision, the people perish: but he that keepeth the law, happy is he." Another translation says it this way, "A hard worker has plenty of food, but a person who chases fantasies ends up in poverty" (NLT). I love this verse because it shows us that vision makes us happy. If you don't have a positive vision for your own life, you will be unhappy, miserable, always seeking acceptance from others, and lonely. God never called us to be this way. He called us to be happy, the head and not the tail, above and not beneath, the lender and not the borrower; therefore, if we are anything other than what God has called for us to be, now is the time to ask God to restore our vision!

This process is very vital for your development as a person and a child of God and can be tough for many reasons. One reason is that a lot of us may have never had a vision for our lives and have been living off the expectations of others. For example, when I was a kid, I desired to be a doctor or a dentist and I loved watching the discovery channel when they had shows that recorded various surgeries and procedures. So, when people would ask me what I wanted to be when I grew up, I would tell them that I wanted to be a doctor or a dentist. There are a lot of people who are like me, but there are some that have never hoped for anything. Maybe you have never had a hope or a desire to be anything beyond yourself. Perhaps you've been scared to dream because of your environment, inadequacies, or lack of support. Maybe you've been afraid to share your dreams with others because you fear they won't understand. I understand how you feel because It's hard to dream for better when you have no one to push you to get there. But there is hope because God is with you, and desires for you to be great, happy, and successful. Josh 1:9(NLT) says, "This is my command—be strong and courageous! Do not be afraid or discouraged. For the Lord, your God is with you wherever you go." This prime understanding is key to our acceptance of our role in life and positions us to walk in our vision. Are you ready?

Where do we start?

Well, we must first understand that all vision comes from God. Even as children, our desires to be great are an inspiration of God's Holy Spirit. God doesn't wait until we get old to begin to show us what we are made of; he starts when we are young and full of energy. There was a story in the bible, where Jesus was separated from his parents' and they were upset when they found him sitting among the teachers in the synagogues - they asked him what he was doing, and he replied, "Why were you searching for me?" he asked. "Didn't you know I had to be in my Father's house?" But they did not understand what he was saying to them." (Luke 2:49-50). Jesus had a vision for his life and he knew he had some business to take care of. He didn't care about his age, stature, or comparison to others; he pursued the vision he had for his life. Now, look at verse 50 because it is vital. Verse 50 says, "But they did not understand what he was saying to them"; this should give you hope because everyone will not understand or even accept the vision you have for your life, not even your family. The people that are closest to you will have the hardest time accepting your vision because they've witnessed your accomplishments and failures and can sometimes fail to believe that you can do better. This can be very discouraging, but you must stay focused on your vision like Jesus and be about your father's business.

4 Phases of Manifesting Your Vision

Understanding that vision comes from God, you must seek him to get it, and sometimes he will show you a glimpse of your future without you having to ask for it. Nevertheless, as you seek God, ask him to show you who you really are and his plan for your life no matter how big or small it is.

This is going to require a lot of faith, patience, reception, and execution from you to see your vision come to reality. It's going to require a lot of faith because; you must believe that God has a vision for to receive it. Hebrews 11: 1(NLT) says, "Faith shows the reality of what we hope for; it is the evidence of things we cannot see," therefore, your faith is the key to receiving things that you cannot see with your eyes. Secondly, this process is going to require patience because God won't always answer your prayers immediately. God often tries our faith by delaying the answers to our prayers to see if we truly believe that he will, but don't worry, because if you keep your faith, God will answer you. As long as you believe that He will, He can!

Thirdly, this process is going to require reception. Reception is the process of receiving or accepting something. This is important because after God has heard your prayers, and you've waited patiently for the answer, he is going to send you the answer and you must be in a position to receive it. It's just like a wide receiver that goes out for a pass but runs the wrong route, ending up in the wrong position. So, we must stay in a place of expectancy, knowing that in due time, God will answer our prayers and give us the plan for our lives. Lastly, the process is going to require execution. After you have sought God for your vision, waited patiently for your answer and received it in your heart, it's time to execute it. The word execute means to do something that you have planned to do or been told to do.

Execution is when your dream becomes a reality. Execution is when your business transfers from your mind to a business card. Or when your recipe goes from your heart to a professionally printed menu. Execution is what makes the process all worth it. If you go through the first three steps, then decide not to execute, you have failed yourself and God. Don't be discouraged or distracted in your process of execution, because your vision isn't just for you; it's also for the people connected to you. Genesis 37 talks about a young man named Joseph, who was favored by his father and given a coat of many colors because he was the youngest, which caused his brothers to hate him. Joseph also had two dreams, which displayed him as a ruler of his people and caused his brothers to hate him even more. So, his brothers decided to get rid of Joseph because of his dreams.

I must tell you that some people aren't going to like you because you dream big dreams. They're going to be highly intimidated by the visions you speak about and try to deter you from executing them, but you must stay focused and love them through it all. Nonetheless, as time progressed, Joseph's brothers sold him to the Midianites, only to be placed in Potiphar's house, and cast into the King's jail. This wasn't because Joseph was an advocate for crime or a menace to society; these things took place because his family didn't want his dreams to come to pass. Therefore, no matter what you go through, stay focused on the vision because a setback is only a set up for your vision to become a reality! So, protect it!

There is a hit out on your Dream!

I'm sorry to tell you, but just like Joseph, there is a hit out on your dream. Have you ever wondered why it's taken you so long to finish the vision that God gave you? Have you ever wondered why there have been so many setbacks and distractions? Well, as children of God, we carry the same DNA and power that Jesus possessed, which makes us prime targets for the enemies' attacks. When King Herod found out that the messiah was being born, he ordered all the midwives to kill every male born child to solidify his status as the ultimate ruler. He knew of the vision that God had for his people and he did everything he could to stop it.

Therefore, as you pursue the execution of your vision, you must be vigilant and very careful about who knows about your vision and who assists in the completion of it. This is very important because the more people that know about your dream, the more people can sabotage it! However, the fewer people that know about your dream, the fewer possibilities it has of being sabotaged. We learn this as we assess the life of Jesus Christ. Jesus was God wrapped in the flesh but kept a low profile. There were certain times when he specifically demanded people to be discreet about the miracles that he performed; however, this wasn't always the case. Jesus also had 12 disciples that followed him during his ministry on earth that he kept secrets from until the time was right. Even when he tried to explain his vision to them, that didn't understand and even didn't believe.

I've experienced this a lot because God has blessed me with a mind that is constantly dreaming and seeking to do great things. Though this has been a major blessing to me, it has also been a curse because I often dream more than I execute. However, when I get locked on to something, I go at it with all my might. Therefore, I often fight against internal discouragements, doubts, insecurities, and limitations because my mind thinks beyond my circumstances. See, God has blessed us to be able to dream ourselves out of poverty, depression, lack, low self-esteem, and bondage – the devil doesn't like that. Joseph's brothers couldn't contain him because he lived according to his vision not according to what he saw. The only thing they saw was their ability to herd the flock and his position of favoritism. It's not your fault that you don't bow down to your circumstances or situations, so you must have enough faith to fight for your dreams no matter the cost. Even if you aren't a dreamer, but you find yourself looking at others wondering if your life could be like theirs; your life can be great as well if you ask God for forgiveness and decide to live the life that God has for you.

The Danger in Blindness

Have you ever walked into a room while the light was off and could not find the light switch? Having to feel your way around, trying not to hit your toe on something caused your awareness to rise but your inability to see still hindered your ability to move. Let me ask you another question: Have you ever been inside of a Haunted house and been terrified by a scary clown or mummy chasing you with a chainsaw? Maybe you were or weren't scared, but it wasn't that the clown himself was scary or you were afraid of what he would do to you. The element of surprise and your inability to see is what made the experience terrifying and unforgettable.

Well I must say that this is the same experience we have in life when we are going about our days working, churching, and having fun without possessing a vision for our lives. We're taking care of our responsibilities and getting things done but we aren't living life to its totality. Often when we're in this state, we feel a sense of hopelessness and subconsciously compare ourselves to other people who seem to be happy and have found their purpose. But deep down inside we're perishing and desiring to have more. I've seen that we often compare ourselves to others and foster a deep resentment for ourselves due to lack of productivity or success in certain areas of our lives. This causes us to develop insecurities and breed thoughts of low self-esteem and depression. Truthfully all of this can be fixed by following the four phases listed above, which are having faith, patience, reception of what God says, and executing the plan.

Noteworthy, as men comparison and image clarification, starts at an early age. Usually, when we start looking up to other men of great renown and stature - then we try to immolate their lives. I remember when I was growing up, everybody wanted to be like Michael Jordan. So, I would try to do his moves, dribble like him, and dunk from the free-throw line but I never made it. I even collected his tradeable basketball cards and watched him on TV but though this was truly something funny happened. Once Michael Jordan retired, I no longer wanted to be like Michael Jordan and started to imitate LeBron James. He was the newest and most dominant player on the court. His moves were fresh, the shot was pure, and dunks were disrespectful, so I began my quest towards walking in the path that he walked in. Now let me pause here to say that there is nothing wrong with admiring a hero or having a mentor that you desire to be like. There is nothing wrong with knowing someone who is currently doing what you desire to do in the future and studying their process to fine-tune yours. However, it gets dangerous when you completely forsake, striving to identify your voice to take on someone else's.

As men, this happens a lot when we get in group settings. When we get around other men, we tend to measure ourselves to others to determine our worth, value, or stature, but I'm here to tell you that you are an amazing man and God has called you to Change the World in your own way. My world-changing journey began while I was on a 6-month deployment out to sea aboard the CVN 69 aircraft carrier named after Dwight D. Eisenhower. This is a humongous naval ship that can fit up to 5,000 people and sustain their living for months.

One day while manning my flight deck position, God began to tell me that I was a World Changer and laid out a plan for my life. He showed me that I would be teaching, speaking, and empowering teens and young adults to enhance their lives and prepare them to be successful. God also gave me the vision to build 'The Hope Center' which will be a youth development center that will provide summer programs, classes, and training in the areas of engineering, computer programming, and nursing. The Hope Center will be available to children and high school students for a small monthly fee. This vision was BIG and very, very, detailed. It was mind-blowing and finally, I felt that I had a purpose in my life and a goal to attain. Now before this moment, I was living simply to survive without any direction, but when God stepped in and opened my eyes, everything changed.

Since the day, and upon my return home, I went to work and God was right with me. As months would by, I got ordained as a minister at my church and began to take on more responsibilities. I started to teach Adult Sunday School Classes, preach on Friday nights, teach Bible Studies, speak at the local YMCA while volunteering with other brothers from the youth development program we started back in 2011. Not only did all of that take place, but God began to give me a book to write titled The Turning Point which is currently finished in my laptop as well as a workbook titled The Purpose Plan, which details a four-step process to help people discover their short and long-term purpose. In recent years I've had the honor and privilege to preach in Lincoln, Alabama and Newport News, Virginia while also leading and overseeing multiple ministries at my local church. One of my greatest and most memorable accomplishments came in 2018 when God gave me the vision to host a Men's Conference titled the Renaissance Man Men's Conference. During this event, we brought in local Pastors, Professors, and experts in the areas of Faith, Men's Health & Wellness, and Financial Development and partnered with local Entrepreneurs, businesses, non-profits, and Regent University to provide men and the local community with information to enhance their lives.

Now let's go back to what I said before: before 2012, I was a new active-duty sailor in the United States Navy and was solely focused on saving money, going to college, and possibly becoming an officer. That was the extent of my vision. There was not much thought put into it. These were things that I knew I needed to survive but had no connection to the development of others. But fast forward to 2012, I had faith and believed God; I was in the right position in my heart, believed what he said, created a plan and executed it. So, I can guarantee that if you follow these four steps, your life will change. I went from surviving to living. From darkness to light. From Blind to sight, only because my heart was in the right position to receive from God and God knew that he could trust me with his desire for my life.

I know we haven't addressed this, but we're going to end on this note: Though it's vital to possess a vision and to execute it you must know that it's just not an idea; it is God's desire for your life. Look at it as God expressing his heart to you when he shows you who you are. Imagine God sitting down in front of, having a conversation with you about his intentions for your life. This is exactly what a vision is. It's not just an idea or mindless thought. It is an expression from heaven that can be backed, funded, and protected by God if you walk in it in obedience.

So, I wonder, has God given you a vision for your life that is great, big, and seems impossible? Has he given you a dream of doing something in the future that does not match your current reality? If so, I understand and I know what it's like to have a dream of being great when you are insecure and unable to see it coming to pass. I know how it feels to be filled with so many ideas but have little to no money. But I want to tell you today, dream again! Trust God! Dust your dream off and pick it back up because God has you reading this book to wake you up and push you to walk in your destiny! Destiny is determined by your ability to trust God beyond your limitations, so now is the time to trust him and go Forward! You are a World Changer! You are a Trendsetter and ultimately, YOU ARE ENOUGH! Love ya Man.

CHAPTER 13
THE CHOSEN ONE: FROM A WHORE TO A MENTOR

1 Samuel 16: 1 (NLT)

Now the Lord said to Samuel, "You have mourned long enough for Saul. I have rejected him as king of Israel, so fill your flask with olive oil and go to Bethlehem. Find a man named Jesse who lives there, for I have selected one of his sons to be my king."

Have you found yourself feeling bad about something that you've done? Well, this was my life for a long time. I used to be out and about, running the streets, hanging with my boys, doing what they were doing, but I wasn't enjoying the experiences as much as they were. Whether it was trying to see who could attract the most ladies, get the most phone numbers or compete on who could have the most sex, within, I knew something was different about me. Although I'd go from one girl to the next, I wasn't willing to stop because my time with them brought me temporary relief and allowed me to escape from the disappointment of my current reality. In this chapter, I'm going to discuss how God took me from being a whore to a mentor, further discussing how He will do the same for you through practical life steps and His powerful Word.

Playa, Playa, Playa!!!

Back in the day, I used to be the man – I had all the girls! Have you ever said, "let me tell you about one girl I used to talk to?" Have you found yourself reminiscing about the "good ole days" or admiring how cool you use to be? I found this to be my truth for a while and I relished in my past pursuits not understanding that the playa I used to be wasn't who God called me to be. Think about who you are today and who you used to be…would you say that you're satisfied with your life or that you find fulfillment in the things that you do?

When I was out doing my thang, I thought it was fun and it gave me joy, but I quickly realized that the joy was temporary and only lasted as long as the intercourse did. But when the moment was over, my happiness faded with it. I believe that many men who are faithful to things, people, and actions that aren't fulfilling their lives. These men have built their lives around people and material possessions to sustain their existence, but these individuals and belongings aren't making them happy. They choose to continue doing such things because they feel that they don't have any other options. Perhaps you may be one who was or is currently tied to something that you desperately desire, but it doesn't make you happy. You may feel trapped – afraid or even so terrified that you're paralyzed to the point that your body and soul seem powerless. I want you to know that you can be FREE and LIVE the life that God has called you to. Here are some practical steps you can take to break free from the past and enter into a new life of possibilities:

✓ Pick up a new hobby (dancing, writing, skydiving)
✓ Adopt a new workout regimen and spend time with friends at the gym
✓ Read your Bible, pray and make a commitment to please God

The Void

This chapter is based on my journey of going from a *whore to a mentor*. I wasn't born addicted to sex, porn, or attention; I was drawn to those worldly things thinking they would fill a *void*. I was hoping to fill the voids of love, acceptance, and satisfaction, which were caused by various negative life experiences and thoughts. My emotions haunted me daily and tormented me nightly in my dreams. I turned to sex, porn, and the attention of others to cope with the weight of these emotions. Though this was my experience, I believe that nowadays in society, it's hard for men to share that they have voids of insecurities, doubts and fears. One reason we can't properly communicate our emotions is because we were never taught how. Statistically, most men aren't raised with fathers in the home or a consistent father figure to show us the way; therefore, as men we aren't able to properly share how we feel because we were never given the blueprint.

Secondly, it's hard for us to share our emotions because traditionally it has been frowned upon; especially in the African American community. Culturally speaking, men who share their emotions are labeled as feminine and can also be mistaken as homosexual. Beloved, this is ignorant and foolish! However, the reality is that some women frown upon men who are confident with sharing their emotions and look at it as a form of weakness. The term *"normative male alexithymia"* describes how some males suffer from culture conditioning that makes them conceal their emotions, which eventually affects their quality of life, as well as, the lives of those closest to them.

Thirdly, it's hard for us to share our emotions because we *fear* being rejected. Therefore, when we can't communicate our deepest feelings which pushes us to turn to exterior outlets – using them as avenues of escape with hopes of receiving temporary peace and satisfaction.

Slaying our fears requires us to change the way we think, which involves a transformation of the mind and choosing to obey God instead of fulfilling our fleshly desires. Regardless of the state you're in, it's not too late to fulfill what God has called you to do.

Make a decision today, right now, not to let your past experiences, disappointments, and failures determine your future. Be committed to living a better life and refuse to waddle in self-pity and defeat. Even if you're a lucrative business owner, model family member, managing the finances of a major company, on the verge of graduating from college, or pastoring a church, change is possible for you. Where you're at right now isn't your final destination, it's merely a step to get you to the divine destiny that God has for you. Here are some practical steps to help you become a better YOU.

- Reality Check: Do a self-evaluation and see yourself for who you are
- Develop a relationship with Jesus Christ
- Forgive, let go of anger, and accept responsibility for your actions
- Identify your passions
- Connect with like-minded brothers
- Be kind and a good listener
- Respect yourself and others'
- Educate yourself
- Write the Vision – set goals
- Manifest the Vision – accomplish the goals

Reality Check: Do a Self-Evaluation and see yourself for who you are

Honestly, I was having fun doing me while I was operating outside the will of God. I had a beautiful girlfriend, lucrative career, decent health, athletic build, savings in the bank, and a promising future. Truth be told, I didn't want for anything, or did I? Blinded by worldly thinking, I thought accruing material possessions that I desired would've been fulfilling, but boy was I wrong. As time progressed and I continued on my path of life, I started to realize that the life that I was living was not as fun as it used to be. I began to realize that I wasn't having fun; I was settling. Looking from the outside-in, I was set, doing well, but from the inside-out I wanted more and needed God to give it to me. Whether you're a Christian or not, take time to evaluate where you are in life and get to know who you are. Are you happy, fulfilled, and energized? If not, you might want to give Christ a chance to show you what life is really about.

Develop a Relationship with Jesus Christ

A priority on my life-list is becoming who God has called me to be – and understanding that a relationship with Christ not only brings new life but empowers us to become victorious in our pursuit of happiness. Even if you already have a relationship with Christ, but have grown weary, lost zeal, or have come to look at church as merely a job rather than a service; you too can be refreshed and start a new life with Christ today. Now, I'm not saying that life before Christ isn't life at all, but it's God's will for His sons to walk in their purpose; therefore, submitting to Christ is the key to breaking away from the old and coming into the new. This *new life* that I'm speaking of is far greater than one could ever think, dream, or imagine and has a way of strengthening your faith and exciting your Christian experience. After giving my life to Christ, my eyes were open to the many possibilities of my future and my desires changed to things that gave me life instead of taking life from me.

Forgive, let go of Anger, and Accept Responsibility for your Actions

Forgiveness is one of the most powerful tools that God has given mankind. You may be wondering, what does forgiveness have to do with going from a *whore to a mentor*? Well, it has a lot to do with it. What if I told you that it was unforgiveness that drove my desire to have sex. Not only was I fostering unforgiveness towards others, but I was also holding unforgiveness towards myself. Unforgiveness is so powerful that if you don't address it, it'll cause you to do things that you never thought you'd do. For example, if you were sexually abused, molested, or raped and you don't forgive the perpetrator, you're likely to repeat the action that happened to you. I'm not saying that this is true for everyone, but many times, those who don't get healed, seek help, or forgive those who've hurt them, often go on to hurt others. I dealt with unforgiveness in my heart for a long time and I urge you to seek help/healing to learn how to forgive those who hurt, abandoned, or rejected you. Letting go of anger and accepting responsibility for where you are in life is a vital step required to move forward and live a prosperous life.

Identify your Passion(s)

Identifying your passions are key to God transforming your life, so what do you like to do? What makes you happy? What would you do for free the remainder of your life? In my case it's mentoring and helping teens. Since I was young, I often found myself helping those in need and asked my mom if those who were less fortunate at my school could come spend the night at our house. This happened a couple of times and it led to a few of my classmates staying at our house for months at a time. This happened in middle school all the way through high school and it was when I noticed that I had a heart to serve. Also, during the summer of my high school years, I worked as a junior mentor and senior mentor for the North Columbus Boys & Girls Club.

This was one of the most amazing jobs that I've had and would later become a hint to what God was calling me to do.

So, with my life as an example, what would you say your passion(s) are? Outside of preaching, teaching, pastoring, fathering, and being a husband or any other responsibility...what makes you smile? I ask these questions because it's those passions that are going to sustain your walk with God when things get hard. Coming into an understanding of what God is calling you to do outside of ministry is going to help bring balance to your life when there are issues going on in the church. Not only that, depending on what your passions are, you may be able to not only serve people but monetize your gifts. How do I know? You are reading this book? I took life, organized it, and created a product.

Writing hasn't always been my passion, but this is another thing that God called me to do after I gave my life to Him and He can do the same thing for you.

Transitioning into a writer is very crucial to understand and can change your perspective forever. Prior to 2012, I had no plans, desires, or vision to be an author – truth be told, I wasn't even good at writing. I hadn't read one book from front to back my entire four (4) years of high school or two (2) years of college. Like most people, I simply read enough to finish or complete an assignment. Reading just wasn't my thing. I didn't read my first book from front to back until I joined the Navy. Therefore, because I wasn't an avid reader, writing was far from my desire; however, God has a way of calling you to do things that you have no background, experience, or skill in. That's one way to receive confirmation that your assignment is called by God for you to fulfill and not just a distraction to prolong your journey.

God has a way of calling men to several things they aren't good at so they can rely solely on him. This was proven in my life and even in one of the strongest men in the Bible – Noah. Nowhere in scripture does it say that Noah had prior experience in shipbuilding. We don't read that he was a master craftsmen, carpenter, or tradesmen. We don't even know what his current occupation was, but we do know that he was considered as honorable, perfect, and 'just' in the eyes of God; therefore, it was those characteristics that God looked at and positioned him to receive the opportunity to build the ark. I say opportunity because God gives man the opportunity to do great things by showing and giving us ideas, visions, and dreams. It's our job to take these things, passions, and desires and bring them to past. Therefore, when God showed me that I would be writing back in 2012, I chose to believe Him and work hard to see this vision come to pass.

Are you a writer, organizer, server, artist, spoken word artist, candle maker, or playwriter? Or are you good at setting order, creating word documents, excel sheets, graphic design, furniture repair, rebuilding cars, cutting grass, laying tile, creating websites, etc.? All these things can be used to expand the Kingdom of God as well as enhance your confidence, and your financial portfolio. Therefore, the sooner you identify your passions, the sooner God can give you a strategy to use them for His good and yours as well.

Connect with Like-Minded Believers

One of the greatest things about our Christian walk is being able to share our experiences with other people. This is the core of our relationship with God because for us to grow we must work together. Hebrews 10:25 states, "And let us not neglect our meeting together, as some people do, but encourage one another, especially now that the day of His return is drawing near" (New Living Translation). Then the Bible says that Iron sharpens Iron, therefore, we need to work together to make each other better. This worked in my life and is the reason behind the title of this chapter.

Back in 2011, me and two brothers from my church were walking out of the gym talking about our passions for mentorship and volunteering. We talked about our past mentorship experiences and our love for organizations like the Young Men's Christian Association (YMCA) and the Boys & Girls Club. I was a member of the Boys & Girls Club for about 8 years of my childhood then later became a paid staff member as a Senior Mentor. I loved working at the Boy & Girls Club; however, after joining the military and leaving my hometown, I was disconnected from that experience and looking for a place to continue in my service.

After leaving the gym with my brothers, we proceeded to my barracks (military housing for sailors and soldiers) to continue our discussion. We decided to start a teen *male* mentorship program. So, we spent the afternoon planning and writing ideas about our future endeavors. We came up with an organization name, motto, scripture, logo, implement exams, colors, and admission requirements. God was in mist and He used us as vessels to bring this vision to His people. After writing the vision, we presented it to our Senior Pastor and asked his permission to start the ministry at church. He excitedly explained to us that he had always desired to start a program like this but did not have the manpower or resources to get it done. Sharing the vision with our Senior Pastor and his response was confirmation of God's approval. After following his instructions and trusting God, *The Chosen Ones*: Teen Male Fundamental Development and Outreach Program was started and is still operating today, by the grace of God.

That was our story – what's yours? What has God shown you that hasn't come to fruition yet? Do you feel limited in your ability to complete the mission God has called you to? What vision do you possess that is so big only God can accomplish it? Is there anyone around you that has what you need to launch your vision off the ground? Have you identified your skillset, gifts, abilities, knowledge, and areas of influence? As a visionary, dreamer, encourager, and one who loves to create programs and tools to benefit others I encourage you to answer those questions and start turning ideas into actions.

My brother Ahmaude is great at setting order, management, and researching. He's also a great supporter, teacher, and spokesman. However, my Brother Ammanuel is a computer genius, and great at creating class type resources, marketing material, testing tools, publishing, writing, and creating scripts, books, and movies. I share this because as you can see, we all have various skill sets and areas of influence, but we shared the same vision. Therefore, by coming together we were able to sharpen each other and make our vision greater.

Plus, we understood our different *callings* and *gifts,* which allowed us to be more productive and efficient when creating the outreach program.

Be Kind and a Good Listener

Be kind to one another, tenderhearted, forgiving one another, as God in Christ forgave you (Ephesians 4:32, ESV). Let me be the first to admit that being kind isn't always easy. Sometimes it's hard to be kind, especially to those who aren't kind to you. Kindness shows others that you care and you could possibly change someone's life by taking a moment to be nice. You never know what a person is going through, especially nowadays when people don't seem to get a break from life-event to the next. This life is fast-paced and filled with tasks and distractions – it's even difficult to have a face-to-face conversation with people for more than 30 minutes and some days individuals don't have time to talk at all.

Think about it, when was the last time that you've actually sat down and listened to someone speak for at least 30 minutes? I wonder how we are communicating nowadays and how will face-to-face communication be in the future. I present these points because being kind and becoming a good listener are all things that I wasn't good at back in my whoring stage. Inconsiderate and selfish used to describe me, but I realized for God to change me, I had to put in some effort and changing my ways was the perfect start. I still struggle with engaging and listening at times, but I've gotten a lot better and I'm proud of the *strong man* that God has created within me.

Respect Yourself and Others

Do you respect yourself? How do you define self-respect? According to Oxford Dictionary, self-respect is defined as "pride and confidence is oneself; a feeling that one is behaving with honor and dignity." Do you treat others with honor and how do you allow people to treat you? Self-respect shapes the way we make decisions in life and is important when it comes to our happiness. Having self-respect can be the deciding factor on how other people perceive you. Knowing your worth and whose you are (God) will prevent a lot of heartache and pain because people won't be so quick to walk all over you.

Understanding your worth and having self-respect reveals the beauty that God already sees in us. The enemy of our souls want to deceive our hearts into believing that we're not who God called us to be, so we must pray and cast all our cares and fears to the Lord. Dismiss negative thinking form your mind and refuse to tolerate physical, mental or verbal abuse form others that don't respect you or themselves. Stand in the Truth of God's Word knowing that you are *chosen, protected, loved, forgiven,* and a *son of God.*

Respecting myself hasn't always been easy. Although, I was taught how to respect my elders and authority figures it was hard learning self-respect. For many years I didn't respect my body which led to putting others in compromising positions with their body. For example, I chose to have sex before marriage which resulted in me putting pressure on others to do the same.

My selfish desires and lack of knowledge opened a door for Satan, who used me to drag my partners down a path leading straight to *hell*. I didn't understand my worth and what God's Word teaches us about our bodies which is a common pitfall that I witness young adults falling prey to often. We must remind ourselves of what God desires for our lives and break the vicious cycle of lacking self-respect. You could possess the solution to teen/young sexual promiscuity by using your gift of speaking or teaching others God's Word and the importance of having self-respect. Be strong and of good courage – chose to fight your flesh and please God. Be the example.

The Importance of Being a Knowledge Seeker – Self-Education

The value of educations is taught to us from an early age. Think back – our parents stressed the importance of earning good grades, graduating high school, attending college, trade-school, or being an apprentice; however, self-education was rarely taught – leading one to believe that in order to receive an education you had to go into debt. Yet, there are several successful people without college degrees who are famous for reaching high levels of success and becoming rich. Have you heard of Bill Gates the founder of Apple or Mark Zuckerberg the founder of Facebook? They were primarily self-educated and equipped with motivation which inspired them to push their selves from one level to the next.

Self-educated people learn in various ways, but they tend to learn little-by-little mastering one single subject at a time. Are you a *knowledge seeker*? If so, your hard work and determination can ultimately lead to success on a personal, financial, or spiritual level. Self-educated people tend to be well-rounded because they seek knowledge in multiple areas of life. Here are some **practical ways** to become a self-educated *knowledge seeker* for little to no cost:

✓ Take free online courses

✓ Attend free workshops

✓ Visit the library and checkout books to educate yourself on topics of interest

✓ Volunteer at church or within your community to gain hands-on experience

✓ Attend Bible Study (Knowledge Seekers Bible Study – Ambassadors for Christ)

Christianity teaches us that God is pleased when we walk in obedience as opposed to how smart we are. Now don't get me wrong, God isn't against education or *knowledge seekers* and the Bible supports this premise by informing us that – the people are destroyed for their lack of knowledge (Hosea 4:6), but if they do not listen, they perish by the sword and die without knowledge (Job 36:12). Therefore, it's no surprise that several of God's followers were well-educated. For example, Moses received the finest education Egypt had to offer and he became mighty in words and deeds (Acts 7:22). Prior to Matthew being a disciple of Christ, he was a publican (tax collector) which is a job that requires training, and some accounting jobs even require educational degrees. So, remember that self-education is a vital part of becoming well-rounded individuals and God expects us to continuously be *knowledge seekers*.

Write the Vision

Writing your ideas and dreams down on paper is one of the most essential things you can do to take your life to another level. This requires much work, effort, and dedication, but if done correctly, can have tremendous positive effects on your life. The Bible tells us in Habakkuk 2:2 to write the vision and make it plain. This truth is important because it shows that in order to write a vision you must first have one.

Living without vision limited my ability to progress and hindered me in such a way that I felt my only option in life was to use my body to get attention instead of using my mind to fulfill my purpose.

When you finish reading this chapter take a moment to look over the chapter titled "I'm a World Changer" which covers the topic of cultivating vision. Ask God to give you His vision for your life and to open your eyes to who and what He has called you to be. Then take time to write what you hear. You don't have to use the standard pen and paper method to jot down your thoughts – get creative and make a vision board. I've made a couple vision boards by using things like tri-boards, peg boards, white boards, magazine cut outs, drawings, scratch paper, staples, and glue. Try to make this process as unique, exciting, and fun as possible put your best ideas into it and remember that this tool will be used to guide you in the pursuits of your dreams, and visions.

Manifest the Vision

Now that you've written your vision, it's time to work on making your dream a reality. If you're anything like me this will be the hard part because coming up with ideas stir-up so much excitement that you want to get it done quickly. Then you're attacked with that fear monster once again which attempts to make you second guess your abilities, skill sets, and insights. Fear comes to distract you and make you doubt your ability to fulfill the visions God gave you. Fear has a way of destroying your zeal and weakening your motivation causing you to want to give up on God and prolong his ability to bless you. 2 Timothy 1:7(NLT) says, "For God has not given us a spirit of fear and timidity, but of power, love, and self-discipline." In this scripture God is sharing with His people that He isn't the one that gives us fear or causes us to be afraid, but He is the one who gives us power, love, and a sound mind.

He is the God that empowers us to walk in his image and declare His name; therefore, fear is of the devil and comes to restrict the Saints from fulfilling the calling over their lives.

Trust me, God wants to us greater vision and He desires for us to fulfill the plans He has for our lives, so we must believe His Word as opposed to the seeds the devil tries to plant in our minds causing us to be paralyzed by fear. God has been speaking to me and giving me visions about entrepreneurship and many other things for years. For example, He has used me to write books and given me opportunities to use my gifts in church as well as in the community. Although I know only God opened some of the doors I walked through – I still questioned God whether the opportunities were God sent which caused me to rely on the military to provide my needs. On August 23, 2018, my faith was tested while on military active duty and I signed contract to remain in the Navy until 2021. This appeared to be the right because it would give me time to finish my bachelors, possibly my masters, publish a few books, start my businesses, and then transition back to being a civilian. However, on August 23rd I was notified that an error found in my service record and I was given an ultimatum and the choices were to reenlist until 2023 or stay in until 2021 with no option of reenlisting if plans changed.

Now that the military was making the rules and I was forced to pick one my life become more difficult than it already was. I felt powerless and because I told everyone my plans, talked to God about getting out in 2021, and had my vision written down – I allowed fear to step in. In an emotionally paralyzed state-of-mind I felt the spirit of the Lord move and remembered to ask my chain of command for a day to pray and deliberate, thank God they showed me favor and gave me the time. I immediately prayed, went home and prayed again, I even took a nap and to ease my mind praying that God would give me a vision in my dreams.

However, later that night I talked to my Apostle and she said "isn't that what you wanted? That's the vision you have written down, so why are you questioning it?" I felt dumb for second-guessing myself and God, but at the same time I was empowered and confident that I was on the right track.

Never feel that you have to settle for what others chose for your life and you don't have to continue living a life that you're not satisfied with. Fulfilling the visions God has given you isn't going to be easy, but if you trust Him and keep the faith you will be prosperous. As for me, I've decided to decline the military's offer and trust the visions God has given me. I'll be starting a new chapter of life in 2021 so stay-tuned to see a **STRONG MAN** rise.

ABOUT THE AUTHOR

Author Robert Vann is a 30-year-old country boy from Columbus, GA who loves God and his People. As a mentor, student, author, motivational speaker, sailor, and minister, Robert Vann thrives off of pursuing his purpose and believes that all people can do the same. He currently serves as an active duty member of the United States Navy wherein he has served 9 years and he also serves as an Elder at Ambassadors for Christ Deliverance Center. As a Student of TCC he obtained 12 Certificates in Non-Profit Management but now attends Regent University pursuing a Bachelors in Christian Leadership & Management. On his free time, Robert is an avid fan of marching bands and drumlines and is new to the dancing scene, learning how to do the Salsa, Bachata, and Moringa. Robert is a true bundle of joy and is fun to be around and hopes to live an inspirational life and leave a positive impactful legacy.

Contact Info:

Facebook: @AuthorRobertbvann

Instagram: @AuthorRobertbvann

Website: www.robertbvann.com

Email: info@robertbvann.com

ACKNOWLEDGEMENTS

To the Strongest Man I know, My Father. Dad I didn't understand before and blamed you a lot for my pain, but now I do. Your sacrifice in serving our country, putting yourself in danger, and being away from your family wasn't to abandon me, but to protect me from experiencing poverty as you had growing up. Though I would've rather had you home, I am forever grateful for your sacrifices and will never forget what you have done! I love you so much and pray that I can be half the man you are! I honor you Sir, Continue to be great.

I also want to say thank you to the greatest Mom in the world. I Love you man! You've been at every game, every band competition, and every chess match. You've been and will forever be my greatest supporter, and for that I'm grateful. I love you mama

Thank you To My...

AFC Family, Apostle Michelle, & Kelly Bowman,

St. Mary's Road United Methodist Church Family,

&

All of My Uncles, Aunts, family, and friends who have poured into me, watched me, prayed for me, dealt with me, disciplined me, and fed me, lol. I love y'all man! We Made it!

To my Team:

Ms. Bridget, Britt, Alyshia, Alicia, Harold, Mike(Bud), & Mykell; If it wasn't for you all, this book would not have happened. Your patience with me and expertise in your areas of skill helped me to just focus on the writing and nothing else. You all wrote this book with me and I want you all to know that you have changed not only my life but everyone who has purchased this book. I love y'all man! We did it!